T0110715

Cambridge Elements ≡

Elements in Publishing and Book Culture
edited by
Samantha Rayner
University College London
Leah Tether
University of Bristol

TRANSLATION IMPERATIVES

African Literature and the Labour of Translators

Ruth Bush

University of Bristol

CAMBRIDGE
UNIVERSITY PRESS

CAMBRIDGE
UNIVERSITY PRESS

University Printing House, Cambridge CB2 8BS, United Kingdom

One Liberty Plaza, 20th Floor, New York, NY 10006, USA

477 Williamstown Road, Port Melbourne, VIC 3207, Australia

314–321, 3rd Floor, Plot 3, Splendor Forum, Jasola District Centre,
New Delhi – 110025, India

103 Penang Road, #05–06/07, Visioncrest Commercial, Singapore 238467

Cambridge University Press is part of the University of Cambridge.

It furthers the University's mission by disseminating knowledge in the pursuit of
education, learning, and research at the highest international levels of excellence.

www.cambridge.org
Information on this title: www.cambridge.org/9781108720045
DOI: 10.1017/9781108766449

© Ruth Bush 2022

This publication is in copyright. Subject to statutory exception
and to the provisions of relevant collective licensing agreements,
no reproduction of any part may take place without the written
permission of Cambridge University Press.

First published 2022

A catalogue record for this publication is available from the British Library.

ISBN 978-1-108-72004-5 Paperback
ISSN 2514-8524 (online)
ISSN 2514-8516 (print)

Cambridge University Press has no responsibility for the persistence or accuracy of
URLs for external or third-party internet websites referred to in this publication
and does not guarantee that any content on such websites is, or will remain,
accurate or appropriate.

Translation Imperatives

African Literature and the Labour of Translators

Elements in Publishing and Book Culture

DOI: 10.1017/9781108766449
First published online: May 2022

Ruth Bush
University of Bristol

Author for correspondence: Ruth Bush, ruth.bush@bristol.ac.uk

ABSTRACT: This Element explores the politics of literary translation via case studies from the Heinemann African Writers Series and the work of twenty-first-century literary translators in Cameroon. It intervenes in debates concerning multilingualism, race, and decolonisation, as well as methodological discussion in African literary studies, world literature, comparative literature, and translation studies. The task of translating African literary texts has developed according to political and socio-economic contexts. It has contributed to the consecration of a canon of African classics and fuelled polemics around African languages. Yet retranslation remains rare and early translations are frequently criticised. This Element's primary focus on the labour rather than craft or art of translation emphasises the material basis that underpins who gets to translate and how that embodied labour occurs within the process of book production and reception. The arguments draw on close readings, fresh archival material, interviews, and co-production and observation of literary translation workshops.

KEYWORDS: translation, literature, Africa, Cameroon, multilingualism

© Ruth Bush 2022

ISBNs: 9781108720045 (PB), 9781108766449 (OC)
ISSNs: 2514-8524 (online), 2514-8516 (print)

Contents

1 Introduction

This book considers the irruptive, embodied, and *felt* dimensions of doing and reading literary translations. Through historical case studies from the Heinemann African Writers Series and analysis of literary translation workshops taking place in Cameroon in 2019, it centres the multidimensional labour and art of literary translators of African texts within structural, sociological, and materialist accounts of the literary field. It does so in order to ask what infrastructure is needed for retranslation and translation to take place, and how and why such translation imperatives continue to matter.

My argument and mixed methodology move between scales of analysis. Chapter 2 challenges the idea of 'translation as metaphor' common in world literature and decolonial theory, and outlines several of the central debates in African literary translation theory/practice that the book then seeks to further elucidate. Chapter 3 delves into archival presences and absences that evoke sociological microhistories of three African and European translators of African literary classics (Simon Mpondo, John Reed, and Clive Wake). It asks how the work of these individuals, against the violent backdrop of decolonisation, played out in the afterlives of these translations: why and how did they come to translate these texts? How have their translations been read? I draw on archives, interviews, and close comparative readings of the translations to probe the limits of archival approaches to African literary history and book history more broadly. Chapter 4 documents more recent imperatives to support literary translators based in Cameroon, who work between English and French within the highly localised context of African language politics and the resurgent Cameroonian Anglophone crisis. Reflecting on the participatory experience of co-producing the Bakwa literary translation workshop in 2019, the chapter unpacks larger issues concerning readership and the politics and pedagogy of literary translation workshops within local and global literary ecologies. It leans on that experience and extant research on counter-hegemonic movements in the contemporary African literary scene to ask what translation and retranslation as a practice of freedom look and feel like in the twenty-first century.

This intervention emerges from institutional contexts in which different kinds of language teaching, as well as literature, humanities, and areas studies teaching, continue to unfold in relation to macro-political contexts of war and peace. Much of my ongoing research and teaching tread a conflicted path between collective projects, redistribution of resources, pedagogical commitments to criticality and hope (in the Freirean sense), and the promotion of a multilingual literary curriculum which remains aware of its own limitations and structural contexts (including the neoliberal university and my lack of fluency in African languages). While based on original primary research, my contributions to debates concerning translation, literature, race, and coloniality in this book are shaped by my embodied experience, languages, and institutional contexts. I will sketch this *habitus* very briefly here, while also acknowledging the necessity and limits of such self-reflexive positioning, especially within participatory research, to which Chapter 4 of the book seeks to contribute.[1]

Like many others, I live my life through translation. Unlike the majority of the world's population, this everyday multilingualism takes place mainly between hegemonic languages: English, French, and Spanish, together with some Wolof and Catalan. My English is, in part, that of a middle-class, white woman who grew up in Northampton, a market town in the middle of England known as the birthplace of Diana Spencer and Doc Martens boots, and, recently, as a stronghold of Brexiteers. Language, like the people and places which shape it, is in constant flux. In a report in the *Guardian* published to profile key young members of the Black Lives Matters protests in July 2020, Tre Ventour, a 24-year-old activist, noted, 'When we protest in Northampton, we're lucky to get 10 people to turn up and we had 1,000 people attend the first Black Lives Matter protest'.[2] Acquired during adolescence and early adulthood spent in Oxford, Paris, and Buenos Aires, my French is mostly Parisian, while my Spanish layers Argentine porteño with the Spanish spoken by my Catalan stepfamily. I benefitted materially from being born in Western Europe to baby boomer, academic

---

[1] In recent decades, feminist and decolonial scholars have led critical reflections on scientific 'objectivity' and provided vital theorisation of the ethics of participatory research. See, for example, Smith, *Decolonizing Methodologies*; Cahill et al., 'Participatory Ethics'.

[2] Mohdin, 'We Couldn't Be Silent'.

parents: a feminist historian mother whose research bridges British women's involvement in imperialism, anti-suffragism, and several decades of work within collective community Black History projects; and a literary translator father, born to a working-class family, who benefitted from the rapid expansion of state-funded secondary and university education in the post–World War II years. My trajectory through state education, with my parental cultural capital, led me to gain three degrees, build a Franco-British family, and secure a permanent university post. These steps, hewn from relative ease of mobility and opportunity, as well as inevitable cultural blind spots, have shaped my literary sensibility, multilingualism, and attitude towards the transformative possibilities of education and research, as well as their hierarchies of knowledge.

The book claims to be neither exhaustive, wholly objective, nor prescriptive as it parses the available archives, interviews, close readings of literary translations, and ethnographic observation of translation workshops. It acknowledges the embeddedness of language and translation within lived, affective contexts that can be glimpsed only obliquely and partially using the dominant research methods in the humanities and social sciences. As the research underpinning the arguments suggests, the literary translators whose labour emerges in the course of the following chapters are enmeshed within the historical, cultural, and social contingencies of their lived contexts. The premise of what follows is that these complex lives, and the people who live them – with hands that choose or decline to scribble, tap, type, and swipe in pursuit of greater social justice and forms of freedom – continue to matter to the ethics and politics of translation as a creative art form.

2 Translation Is Not a Metaphor

In February 2021, the story of a decision by the Dutch poet Marieke Lucas Rijneveld to renege on their contract to translate *The Hill We Climb* – a collection by the poet Amanda Gorman – made international headlines.[3] Pitched in simplistic, racialised terms, Rijneveld appeared to have capitulated to social media polemic and pressure over their capacity, as a white person, to translate poetry by Gorman (an established African American poet who had recently performed her poetry at President Joe Biden's inauguration). The story provoked prolific responses and discussion among translating communities online, in private mailing lists, and in professional forums such as the Translators Association and Society of Authors. An initial consensus emerged that this decision stemmed from Rijneveld's lack of experience as a translator, rather than their racialised identity. Elsewhere, writers suggested that the decision amplified racist rhetoric and polarising language of identity to which literary production should be immune. In a comment video published on Twitter, Alain Mabanckou argued – in line with the familiar universalising discourse of the *littérature-monde* movement – that literature 'grows because it crosses borders. Literature should not be the tributary of a certain colour.'[4]

This rare global North media focus on literary translation as craft and a politically meaningful act dwelt on the stark visibility of translators as human beings with a defined role in the process of book production, rather than necessary but shadowy and depoliticised, preferably invisible, mediators. The fast-flowing responses soon noted the relative absence of black literary translators in the structures of the global literary field. The American Literary Translation Association stated that 'the foundational problem this controversy reveals is the scarcity of Black translators and other translators of color, a scarcity caused by long-term patterns of discrimination in education and publishing'.[5] The long-term practical

---

[3] Reports were published by *Le Monde*, *NRC Handelsblad*, *De Standaard*, *El País*, *CNN*, and the *Guardian*.

[4] My translation. Alain Mabanckou on Twitter, 6 March 2021.

[5] American Literary Translation Association, 'Statement on Racial Equity'.

consequences of such institutional diagnoses are unclear. The choice of translator (just as with Biden's own choice of Gorman) is 'part of the message', one commentator argued.[6] This scarcity was what the Turkish translator Canan Marasligil described as the choice 'not to care' when it comes to the material dimensions of changing the publishing industry.[7] Here, an ethics of care is about bypassing profit-driven motivations, taking the time, and committing the resources that it takes to gradually shift embedded industry norms and networks. Such care is not an easy way to work. Yet these ethics are found in the self-ascribed terms of many literary activists based on the African continent who focus on building infrastructure and meaningful networks of community, in ways which remain fragile, at times fleeting, or unsustainable according to norms of the 'Western Industrial Publishing Complex'.[8]

This highly visible, symptomatic transatlantic case raises some of the theoretical and practical issues tackled in this book. However, the Gorman case runs in a separate groove, given its embeddedness in publishing circuits of the global North. In what follows, I discuss the relationship between literary translation, race, and coloniality in African literary production from the 1950s to the present day. The book does not pin inevitably reductive categories of identity to literary meaning or to the legitimacy or fidelity of the act of translation.[9] It does seek, however, to connect histories and lived experiences of racism and coloniality to structures within the literary marketplace and their consequences, in particular forms of education, pedagogy, mentorship, and networking on which literary production – and aspects of literary form – also depend. In turn, it highlights initiatives which are already redressing the invisibility and under-resourcing of literary translators based on the African continent. The discussion of multilingualism and literary translation thereby seeks to foreground 'the relationship of literary praxis to language

---

[6] Kotze, 'Translation Is the Canary'. [7] Marasligil, 'Uncaring'.
[8] Bwa Mwesigire, 'What Is Literary Activism?', p. 11.
[9] For further discussion of this point, see Galliand, ed., *Faut-il se ressembler pour traduire*, in particular the chapter by Édith Félicité Koumtoudji.

as situated social practice'.[10] This opening chapter lays out several of the key theoretical debates and terms which will be elucidated in the following chapters: translation as (decolonial) metaphor; the literary commons; untranslatability and retranslatability; and translation as activism. It offers provocation for those relatively new to these topics. For those familiar with these ideas, it gives an indication of how this book intervenes in the overlapping disciplinary areas of Literary Studies, Book History, and Translation Studies.

Metaphors and the Literary Commons

Translation remains a central metaphor in literary debates, for which the creative, hermeneutic labour of literary translators is the underlying premise. Broadly speaking, there are two poles to these myriad debates. The first rests upon a commodifiable, anthologised notion of world literature as that which 'gains in translation' and encourages the perceived ethical benefits of reading across national borders through translation.[11] The second emphasises untranslatability, violence, and rupture in the circulation of literary form and meaning.[12] This may be through analysis of the ethics and aesthetics of incommensurability (i.e. the right to *not* be translated or understood, or to retain foreign 'accent' and 'unsettle innocence'),[13] as well as historically informed discussion of institutional and state power.[14] It has become common, however, to acknowledge untranslatability in ways which are detached from the material realities of literary production and circulation, especially as experienced in Southern literary and linguistic contexts. Recent critical engagements with world literature describe such metaphorical takes on translation and untranslatability as a 'political kneecapping'.[15] Indeed, they are symptomatic of

---

[10] Gilmour and Steinitz, *Multilingual Currents*, p. 5.
[11] Damrosch, *What Is World Literature?*, p. 281. For an insightful critique, see Harrison, 'World Literature', p. 421.
[12] Samoyault, *Traduction et violence*.
[13] Coetzee, *Accented*, pp. 5–6; Tuck and Yang, 'Decolonization', pp. 28–36.
[14] Apter, *Against*; McDonald, *Artefacts*, p. 28; Brouillette, *Underdevelopment*.
[15] Venuti, *Contra*, p. 77.

material structures and implicit hierarchies of aesthetic value that determine literary culture itself, from the rise of print to the intersection of literacy and development under European coloniality/modernity.[16] More helpful than the 'untranslatable' or further examples of colonial linguistic violence in the context of the current study, I want to suggest, is the need to centre conditions needed for translation and *re*translation, especially by translators located on the African continent, to become reality. This speaks to Tuck and Yang's salutary reminder, in the context of settler colonialism, that 'decolonization is not a metaphor' but an ongoing process of transforming material realities, in particular the repatriation of Indigenous land and life.[17]

Beyond the literary space, translation is a generative and optimistic metaphor in the many threads of Africa-centred and decolonial theory/ practice which consider extractive dynamics of knowledge production while seeking avenues towards epistemic justice. Ato Sekyi-Otu's suggestion that translation has been integrated as a key resource in a 'civil commons', and is not a site or a priori *source* of universalism, is a particularly useful starting point for my analysis in what follows.[18] His defence of 'left universalism' recuperates the notion of universal ethics in relation to selected African contexts, thought systems, and their 'variegated tongues', rather than 'an alien Kantian cosmopolitan imagination'. This argument emphasises the need not to rely upon a pole of absolute relativism or Eurocentric uni-versalism but to foreground – in a non-exclusionary manner – the universal dimensions of African thought and lived experiences and navigate such middle ground in all its complexity.[19] Boaventura de Sousa Santos makes a related theoretical argument when proposing that 'intercultural translation is the alternative both to the abstract universalism that grounds Western-centric general theories and to the idea of incommensurability between cultures'.[20] Elsewhere, translation expresses forms of hope and optimism and resonates with desire – what Souleymane Bachir Diagne describes as

---

[16] Brouillette, 'On Some Recent Worrying'.

[17] Tuck and Yang, 'Decolonization', p. 21.

[18] Sekyi-Otu, *Left Universalism*, pp. 16, 65.

[19] See also Fraiture, 'Translating African Thought'.

[20] Sousa Santos, *Epistemologies*, p. 212.

a resolutely pan-African, but non-essentialising, 'desire for Africa'.[21] The pursuit of epistemic justice as a pathway to planetary repair depends fundamentally on these affective qualities.

Decolonisation is not an immanent property of translation. The action of translating and reading in translation can contribute to what Ngũgĩ wa Thiong'o terms 'decolonizing the mind', but this does not occur of its own accord. The use and/or learning of multiple languages are embedded in messy power hierarchies, as the recent collectively written 'Short Manifesto for Decolonising Language Education' recalls:

> The mess we have made, of peoples, land, languages, of rivers and of the air is no respecter of nationally drawn postcolonial boundaries and any decolonising foreign language pedagogy worth its salt will need to remember the intimate connections between land, language, and its need of the air for speech, any speech, anywhere, to find articulation.[22]

This need of the air for speech in any language, that is, of clean, pollution-free air that vibrates through the vocal chords or channels oxygen to blood cells to drive fingers to tap on keyboards, resonates with the project of building a multilingual literary commons in the post-anthropocentric moment. I argue in what follows that the idea of a literary commons which acknowledges translation as an embodied form of labour has significant pedagogical, epistemological, and methodological consequences in decolonial approaches to knowledge production.[23]

The 'commons' is a term used in social and political theory to refer to the distribution and management of resources. In the current context of climate crisis, structural inequalities, and historical, social, and epistemic injustice, it has helpful implications for the analysis of social and cultural production. The 'literary commons' is a horizon (i.e. an imagined goal, akin to that of

---

[21] Diagne and Amselle, *In Search.* [22] Phipps et al., 'A Short Manifesto', p. 8.

[23] I adopt here the conflation of theory/practice proposed by the Latin American school of decolonial thought (Mignolo and Walsh, *On Decoloniality*, p. 7).

a truly universal 'universality') for how the resources needed to produce written literature (from time and alphabetical literacy to paper, computer hardware, internet connectivity, and data costs, as well as linguistic and cultural knowledges) might be distributed and managed. The term refers to the material means by which the labour undertaken by writers, literary translators, publishers, and readers can propel new understandings of the world through creative expression. The term's utopian dimensions seem glaring when pitched against the deeply unequal material realities of the world literary space. That space is defined by its contested institutional histories, and the forms of political, cultural, and linguistic violence that continue to prevail in the early twenty-first century. However, this book maintains the ethical need for that horizon, and its associated efforts, as a form of resistance to critical cynicism and in recognition of the powerfully pragmatic work – much of it digital in scope – of the current generation of literary activists based on the African continent.

Several inherently – though at times covertly – optimistic theoretical discussions of the 'commons' frame the ensuing discussion.[24] Altruism and collective action, underpinned by an emphatic recognition of shared humanity, are fundamental to several concepts in African philosophical thought, from Ubuntu to Afrotopia.[25] Such ideas are readily articulated by literary activists currently working on the continent in partial response to the neoliberal logics of the global literary marketplace.[26] Hardt and Negri acknowledge that the 'commons' encompasses 'those results of social production that are necessary for social interaction and further production, such as knowledges, languages, codes, information, affects and so forth'.[27] Literary translation stands as the epitome of the imaginative questing after an ideal 'common' experience necessary to more just kinds of social production. It is the crafted articulation of linguistic and cultural differences.

---

[24] See Ostrom, *Governing*; Hardt and Negri, *Commonwealth*. [25] Sarr, *Afrotopia*.
[26] Bwa Mwesigire, 'What Is Literary Activism?'; Krishnan and Wallis, 'Podcasting', pp. 10–11.
[27] Hardt and Negri, *Commonwealth*, p. viii.

It follows that this book contributes to long-standing discussions among translators and Translation Studies scholars concerning literary translation as a form of activism which 'stirs readers and audiences to action'.[28] This activist approach also challenges metaphorical takes on translation as a form of bridge-building between linguistic cultures. It has signalled complex forms of violence, ethnocentrism, and racism that translation can enact in conscious and unconscious, deliberate and accidental, individual and structural ways. In turn, activist translators and translation scholars foreground the role of translation and interpreting in zones of conflict and highlight the work of activist translator collectives.[29]

Contextualising Untranslatability and Retranslatability

In its focus on the contingency and historicity of literary translation, the present study considers multilingualism as something which 'has no fixed valency: it may serve dominant visions of the nation-state, or cosmopolitanism, or the effects of global cultural exchange, or unsettle them profoundly'.[30] The transition between languages registers social relations as dimensions of a text's literary form, such that form cannot be disentangled from so-called external readings of texts.[31] These relations are firstly evoked by intratextual translation, as amply explored by scholarship on the translation of African languages, knowledges, and oral cultures into literature written in European languages.[32] They also include relationships of structural domination (gender, race, sexuality, class) manifested through institutional contexts guiding the choice of text and of translator. Lastly, translated texts manifest social relations based on forms of care and shared humanity, however compromised by the aforementioned inequities: the challenges of solidarity; recognition of the translating self and of another human subjectivity; communal joy, laughter, and expressive freedom

---

[28] Gould and Tahmasebian, *Routledge Handbook of Translation and Activism*, p. 4.

[29] Baker, 'Translation and Activism', pp. 462–84.

[30] Gilmour and Steinitz, *Multilingual Currents*, p. 6.

[31] See Harris and Hållén, 'African Street Literature', pp. 3 5.

[32] Bandia, *Translation*, p. 180; Julien, 'African Novels', pp. 26–42; Kane, *Roman africain et tradition*; Quayson, *Calibrations*, p. xiv.

(fleeting though this may at times appear). Here, we might note Tuck and Yang's reminder that 'solidarity is an uneasy, reserved, and unsettled matter that neither reconciles present grievances nor forecloses future conflict'.[33]

The theory/practice of translation is intimately connected to the perennial language question in African literature: which language do or *should* writers use? Sociologists have highlighted how patterns of literary translation in the global literary field perpetuate hierarchies and uneven structural relationships, maintaining the dominance of certain 'global' languages such as English, French, and Spanish.[34] In the African literary space, these trends are amplified further, with books written in former colonising languages representing the vast majority of those consecrated as 'classics'.[35] This has been further echoed in discussion of the dominance of certain genres, though particular textual forms, popular print cultures, and political projects cannot be made to fit neatly into a schematic model and future-oriented temporality of Herderian vernacular nationalism.[36] This is of particular resonance for the case of Cameroon, with its official bilingualism, historically marginalised anglophone minority, and dense everyday multilingualism (more than 250 languages are spoken). It necessitates careful unpacking of how literary translation operates as a process of friction and discontinuity in a context of conflict.

Further to the vitality of debates concerning African languages, colonial language barriers have not been inimical to projects of political and cultural pan-Africanism. Pioneering pan-African or Third Worldist periodicals such as *Présence Africaine*, *Black Orpheus*, *Lotus*, and *Abbia* depended on the collective labour and pragmatic commitment of translators and editors, several of whom were women and remain obscured in existing critical histories.[37] Translation was driven by an immediate concern with delivering

---

[33] Tuck and Yang, 'Decolonization', p. 3.

[34] Casanova, *The World Republic*; Sapiro, 'Translation and Symbolic Capital'; Sapiro and Heilbron, 'Outline'.

[35] Ducournau, *La fabrique*; Intrator, *Books Across Borders*, pp. 109–24; Brouillette, *UNESCO*, ch. 1.

[36] Warner, *Tongue-Tied Imagination*, pp. 206–11.

[37] Reza, 'African Literary Journals', pp. 168–96.

content urgently to readers. It is notable, however, that concerted discussion of literary translation was not on the agenda at the 1956 First Congress of Black Writers and Artists, the 1962 Makerere Conference for writers of African expression, or the colloquium of writers and academics which took place in Dakar in 1963. Indeed, Ousmane Sembène's intervention at the Dakar colloquium suggests that translation was an inconvenient obstacle rather than a matter needing urgent intellectual attention and with the potential to foster forms of engaged solidarity.[38] Significant translation labour also underpinned Afro-Asian literary initiatives in the period of decolonisation, as 'a propagandistic initiative of the Soviet government', and through the landmark trilingual, Third Worldist magazine *Lotus*.[39] This contributed to Cold War translation strategies that diverged from those of large, profit-driven Northern publishing houses.

The matter of language choice and self-justification faced by many contemporary African writers is well-trodden ground, eliciting polemics, fatigue, and at times irritation.[40] These debates have been shaped by divergent political contexts concerning the use of what are alternately called 'national', 'African', 'vernacular', 'local', 'indigenous', or 'endogamous' languages across the African continent. As Tobias Warner has demonstrated, the language question has a tendency to become a 'zombie debate' which reductively pits essentialist/nativist projects against cosmopolitan ideals of multilingualism, or which conflates the myriad literary uses of French with the political project of *la Francophonie*. If posed in different, transhistorical, terms, however, the language question has the potential to reinvent and reignite the literary itself as a transformative realm whose expressivity registers forms of freedom and possibility for differently sited readerships.[41]

Ngũgĩ wa Thiong'o's defence of African languages and Boubacar Boris Diop's writing and translation into Wolof, alongside more recent initiatives such as the *Jalada* Translation Issue, the Ituika platform, and the work of

---

[38] Warner, *Tongue-Tied Imagination*, pp. 1–3.

[39] Djagalov, *From Internationalism*, pp. 107–8; Halim; Popescu, *At Penpoint*, pp. 87, 152.

[40] Boum, 'La francophonie', n.p.; Miano, *L'impératif*.

[41] Warner, *Tongue-Tied Imagination*, pp. 4, 241.

translator-activists such as Wangui wa Goro, Bienvenu Sene Mongaba, Edwige Dro, and Sika Fakambi, have generated admiration and praise. In the digital era, African literary translation manifests new signs of optimism and momentum. Online and print periodicals including *Modern Poetry in Translation*, *Retors*, *Words Without Borders*, *Warscapes*, *Asymptote*, *Bakwa*, *Saraba*, *Jalada*, and *Chimurenga* regularly carry translations of African texts by Africa-based and non-Africa-based translators.[42] Literary translation workshops have taken place in a number of African countries, including Mozambique, Kenya, and Cameroon.[43] These initiatives sit alongside a nest of complex and long-running arguments that African language advocacy may reinforce forms of nativism or exclusionary nationalism.[44] Language changes and adapts. It did so with the formation and expansion of languages such as Kiswahili and Lingala, and it continues to so with the development of new forms, pidgins, and creoles, such as the urban Wolof spoken in Dakar (with its borrowings from French and English), Nouchi in Côte d'Ivoire, or Camfranglais in Cameroon.[45] In African literary translation, notions of fidelity and equivalence or hermeneutic and instrumentalist approaches also connect to developmentalist, capitalist, and evangelical ideologies and anxieties that underpin the history and extractive logic of alphabetic and functional literacy on the continent (see Chapter 4).

Theoretical exploration of 'untranslatables' – fascinating though it remains – is untenable as an ethical or practical endeavour in the literary realm without adequate acknowledgement of the historical conditions and infrastructure that enable the process of (re)translation to take place.[46]

---

[42] *Asymptote* currently waive their (controversial) submission and editing fees for contributors based in Africa or translating work from African countries.

[43] Tamele, 'Developing'.

[44] Marzagora, 'African-Language Literatures', pp. 41–2; Kiguru, 'Language and Prizes'.

[45] See Vakunta, 'On Teaching'.

[46] I extend here from Wozny and Cassin's definition in the context of African language translations of the terms 'museum' and 'heritage'. They describe untranslatables as symptoms 'of what is always in the course of being translated' where languages are 'not simply considered as ways of seeing the world but as ways of making it' (*Les intraduisibles*, p. 102). See also Diagne, *L'encre*, pp. 33–7.

Materialist and book-historical approaches seek a fuller, empirical account of the role of institutions and literary mediators, including publishers, booksellers, reviewers, and readers, in the production of notions of literary taste and value.[47] While alert to current work in machine translation, this book foregrounds the imperative to engage with multilingual and transcultural labour in all its complexity. The decision to refuse to translate or gloss terms from indigenous African languages occurring mid-flow in English or French, especially at a time characterised by inexorable appeals to digital connectivity, speaks more helpfully to translation for densely multilingual African readerships than an abstract notion of untranslatability. This key reparative move is found in paratextual decisions by translators and publishers to target readerships based on the African continent by not italicising endogenous terms or providing glossaries and extensive footnotes.

Three brief examples from the contrasting contexts of South Africa, Cameroon, and Rwanda provide suggestive avenues for reflection. Carli Coetzee argues in connection to the post-apartheid context of South Africa that 'translation may at times not serve the best interests of those who are translated, nor of those who perform the labour'. Seen through this lens, translation is 'a site of conflict, rather than a path to reconciliation and understanding'.[48] Here, linguistic 'accent' and the kinds of friction this displays, in subtle and not-so-subtle ways, bypass pre-emptively celebratory accounts of translation's capacity to enact change or forge solidarities. In Cameroon, Joseph Che Suh's analysis of Guillaume Oyono Mbia's self-translated English edition of his classic play *Trois prétendants . . . un mari* (1960) explores Oyono Mbia's use of loan words from Bulu. Suh's discussion signals the textual implications of a shared source and target culture for the play's primary audiences in Cameroon. He notes that the 'cushioning devices' used in the English translation, including stage directions, 'shed only minimal light on the meanings of the Bulu words' and assume shared social realities among the anglophone and francophone Cameroonian audiences.[49] Such critical insight derives from close analysis of African

---

[47] Much of this work draws on the ideas and sociological concepts developed by Pierre Bourdieu. See Bush, *Publishing*, pp. 14–23.

[48] Coetzee, *Accented*, pp. 5–6. [49] Suh, 'Methodological Issues', pp. 157, 161.

literary translation informed by endogenous linguistic knowledge.[50] Elsewhere, Zoe Norridge's French–English translation of Yolande Mukagasana's memoir of the 1994 genocide against the Tutsi in Rwanda, *Not My Time to Die* (published by Kigali-based Huza Press, edited by Doreen Baingana), explicitly connects its African-reader-centred translation and editorial strategies to memory work. In her afterword, Norridge notes that 'our most important audience for the translation, is Rwandans themselves. This informed many of our choices. For example, in the French edition most proverbs are given only in translation, but in this new edition, Yolande and I decided to return to the original Kinyarwanda alongside English translations.'[51] These examples highlight the freedom to choose how to translate (or not) and package translations in particular reparative ways. As Suh argues, this necessitates holistic, empirical recognition of the exercise of readers' agency at local scales.[52]

Further to the theory/practice of literary translators and self-described literary activists, Translation Studies is an established disciplinary area in some parts of the African continent, with particular strength in countries where professional translation, interpretation, and official multilingualism have been integral to the nation-building project, such as Cameroon and South Africa.[53] It is clear that Translation Studies is no longer a Eurocentric disciplinary area, shaped primarily by traditions of Bible translation, the impact of two world wars on code-switching expertise and formalised language education, and the emergence of translation as a key political-economic imperative with the launch of the European Economic Community and its commitment to maintaining its official languages.[54] The institutional growth of Translation Studies as an academic discipline

---

[50] Ibid., p. 157. [51] Norridge and Mukagasana, *Not My Time*, p. 196.

[52] Suh, 'Methodological Issues', p. 147.

[53] Inggs and Wehrmeyer, *African Perspectives*, p. 3. See also the work of the South African Translators' Institute and East Africa Interpreters and Translators Association. It is beyond the scope of the present study to consider intersections with the path-breaking translation traditions and current activities in Egypt, Tunisia, Algeria, and Morocco.

[54] Tymoczko, *Enlarging Translation*, pp. 3–8.

has been further bolstered by the creation in 2016 of the Association for Translation Studies in Africa, following a number of summer schools, and the founding of its associated *Journal for Translation Studies in Africa*, edited by Kobus Marais and published in open access online for the first time in 2020. This journal promises to further much-needed research on translation theory/practice predating European colonialism. Published as this Element was nearing completion, the Routledge edited volume *African Perspectives on Literary Translation*, edited by Judith Inggs and Ella Wehrmeyer, offers a further valuable set of avenues into the theory and practice of literary translation on the African continent (in particular its Southern region).

As will be discussed further in Chapter 4, literary translation has remained under-professionalised as a creative practice on the continent, despite widespread expertise and training courses in professional translation.[55] Cameroon has a strong infrastructure for translation training (there are three MA courses in translation at universities in Cameroon, including the specialist translation training institutes the Advanced School of Translators and Interpreters (ASTI) and L'Institut Supérieur de Traduction, d'Interprétation et de Communication (ISTIC)). While many translation students in Cameroon write on literary translation for their dissertations, most go on to work as translators of legal and technical texts. Translation and interpreting were historically embedded in the power hierarchies of nineteenth- and early twentieth-century colonial projects. The relationship between coloniality, literacy, and religious activity is very much still alive, though it remains relatively marginal in the aesthetic hierarchies of value that characterise academic debates over world literature. In practical terms, literary translation has remained contingent on external grant-funding, passion projects, and an economy of good will. The professionalisation of literary translation as it has occurred in the anglophone global North (where few literary translators make a living from that activity alone but participation in translation summer schools and MA programmes has expanded rapidly) has not so far occurred in step with the expansion of publishing houses based on the continent.

---

[55] See discussion of Collins in Chapter 4.

The rest of this book is structured in two chronological chapters. Chapter 3 unpacks the political and aesthetic dimensions of the labour of three early translators of African literary 'classics'. By considering the circulation of translated poetry by David Diop and Léopold Sédar Senghor in print and performance, it suggests that, despite relative invisibility on a global scale and limited resources, these translators worked in contrastingly creative and liberatory ways. Chapter 4 builds on the collective experience of co-producing a literary translation workshop in Cameroon with the Bakwa collective. It asks what translation and retranslation as a practice of freedom might look like and feel like in the twenty-first century. It does this by highlighting some of the informed, networked modes of optimism which characterise current (re)translation imperatives on the African continent.

3 'Mere Translation!' Rereading Multilingual Labour in the Heinemann African Writers Series

This chapter considers the translation strategies and working practices of two of the most prolific translators of francophone African literature, Clive Wake and John Reed, alongside those of a largely forgotten translator of francophone African poetry, Simon Mpondo, who co-translated (with Frank Jones), David Diop's incendiary anti-colonial collection *Coups de pilon*. By considering the circulation and reception of translated poetry by David Diop and Léopold Sédar Senghor in print and performance, I explore the extent to which these literary translators worked in creative and liberatory ways. Their labour harboured optimism, despite cultural blind spots, contexts of coloniality, and extractive logics which saw the publication of African literature for the school market generate profits for Northern publishing houses such as Oxford University Press, Heinemann, and Indiana University Press. The chapter's comparative dimension aims to highlight the institutional power structures (publishers, universities, Cold War funding for cultural work) which framed this literary translation activity.

A small handful of translators translated francophone African texts into English for publication during the African literary boom of the 1960s and 1970s. This group, most of whom also worked in literature, languages, or extramural departments of African universities, included Abiola Irele, Adrian Adams, Clive Wake, Gerald Moore, John Reed, and Dorothy Blair.[56] They published translations in flourishing series aimed at the African school market, including the Heinemann African Writers Series, Oxford's Three Crowns series, and Longmans. In total, the African Writers Series, founded in 1962 with Chinua Achebe at the editorial helm, published 247 titles in large print runs of orange

---

[56] For a comprehensive account of Blair's translating work, see Steemers, *Francophone African*, pp. 153–5. Blair's archive is housed at the University of Westminster and includes correspondence with authors she translated, including V. Y. Mudimbe, Assia Djebar, and Aminata Sow Fall.

paperbacks.[57] Of these, twenty-seven were translations from French. Some were original commissions, while others were translations already published by American publishing houses. Scholarship on the African Writers Series has highlighted an 'exploitative' commercial logic serving the economic interests of a publisher located in London, while scholarship on the Oxford Three Crowns series signals how Oxford University Press was able to subsidise other branches of its scholarly publishing using profits from contracts to supply the African school market.[58]

My argument is literary, historical, and methodological in scope. It broaches the history of British expatriate university teaching in Southern Africa, transatlantic racial politics of the 1960s and 1970s, and necropolitical realities in post-independence Cameroon. In view of extant scholarship on the translations by Reed and Wake, the comparison with Mpondo also aims to expose the methodological pitfalls of archival work in book-historical research. It notes the tendency to reproduce (albeit critically) colonial power and white agency rendered visible by abundant print archives and demonstrates how this asymmetry can be tempered. I emphasise the need to attend to traces of translators' agency located within the literary texts themselves, as well as ephemera and oral history, as a way of balancing archival volume.

Murderers and Proles?

Translation theory has amply elucidated the interpretive task of translation, the relationship of 'source' to 'target' language, and tropes of equivalence, fidelity, and freedom. It has increasingly sought to unpack translators' strategies in relation to sociopolitical and cultural contexts and through the prismatic effect of non-standardised languages, intermedial influence, and the fluidity of electronic texts. Detailed literary and sociological analysis of early translations of African literary classics and frequent anecdotal

---

[57] This series has been the subject of extensive scholarship on coloniality and canonicity. Those arguments will not be rehearsed here. See, for example, Lizarríbar, 'Something Else'; Currey, *Africa Writes*; Ibironke, *Remapping*.

[58] Bejjit, 'The Publishing'; Davis, *Creating*.

references (see Chapter 4 in the present study) have pinpointed examples of cultural mistranslation that occur when a translator's life experience does not map onto that of the author.[59] Such critiques pertain to a perceived removal or loss of something integral to the source text, whether its form or – more frequently – specific cultural references. John Reed's translations of Ferdinand Oyono's novels are a case in point. Paul Bandia criticises Reed's rendering of Oyono's characters' 'broken French' in *Houseboy*. These dialogues are translated into an approximated 'broken English', rather than the codes and lexicon of West African Pidgin Englishes.[60] Elsewhere, Femi Ojo-Ade describes Reed as a 'murderer of the message' whose 'mangled' translation of *Une vie de boy* (Houseboy) signals a neocolonial power pact between British publisher and translator.[61] Ojo-Ade suggests, 'as a white man, the translator's sympathy lies with the colonialists vilified by Toundi, the houseboy'.[62] His essay lists numerous errors and idiosyncrasies (children for *petits nègres*; drawers for *pantalon*; stick for *chicotte*) and stylistic difference between the source and target text. Exclamations become dulled, and unpunctuated remarks and ellipses signalling silences or lack of response in conversations are removed. Most recently, Felix Awung has conducted a valuable sociological study of these translations in relation to Reed's personal 'habitus' and position in the literary field, drawing on Bourdieusian tools and email interviews with Reed, which the current chapter seeks to supplement.[63] Reed and Wake published seven volumes of poetry translation as well as novels and dramatic texts by authors including Seydou Badian, Mongo Beti, Ferdinand Oyono, and Malick Fall.[64] Wake provided many reader's reports for Heinemann and Oxford University Press, vetting translations done by others over several decades. Awung, Ojo-Ade, and Bandia expose forms of linguistic and cultural friction that obtain in these translations, in part due to

[59] Bandia, *Translation*, pp. 99–101; Awung, 'Translating', pp. 254–5.

[60] Bandia, 'On Translating', p. 110. [61] Ojo-Ade, *On Black Culture*, pp. 155–62.

[62] Ibid., p. 157. [63] Awung, 'Representing'.

[64] Reed and Wake, *A Book of African Verse*; Senghor, *Prose*; Reed and Wake, *Anthology*; Senghor, *Nocturnes*; Reed and Wake, *French African Verse*; Rabéarivelo, *Translations*; Reed and Wake, *A New Book of African Verse*.

the positioning and cultural competence of the translator. As I will develop further in Chapter 4 of this book, their studies provide ample grounds for the urgent retranslation of these (and other) African literary classics.

Translation can erase forms of cultural difference, repackaging a text in ways which centre the source-text reader and instate aesthetic norms without being mindful of diverse contexts of reception. The process of translation is not innately violent, however. Such repackaging can be consciously political and emancipatory, drawing on anti-colonial and anti-racist principles. Kaima Glover, for example, writes of the 'high-stakes' process in her work translating the Haitian author René Depestre, stressing the task of translating Haitian blackness within pre-existing and overdetermining global narratives associated with Haitian history and religious practice. She describes her intention to translate 'to and for a desired Afro-diasporic readership' and the 'destigmatizing effort' involved in this task to 'create space for an expanded notion of blackness within the African diaspora'.[65] More broadly, the structural occlusion of translators of colour remains symptomatic of a literary system governed by dominant regimes of aesthetic taste (namely Euro-American literary modernism). What, then, did the labour of literary translation involve and symbolise during the period of formal decolonization? I use the term 'labour' deliberately here, rather than a Benjaminian 'task', to foreground the material dimensions of literary translation and structural contexts of Reed's, Wake's, and Mpondo's relative visibility or invisibility.

An approach attuned to forms of structural inequality and embodiment grounds the suggestion, derived from post-structuralist critique, that all translation is interpretative, contingent, or subject to endless retranslation (i.e. it is 'untranslatable'). In her 'Twenty Theses on Translation', which range from 'Nothing is translatable' to 'Everything is translatable', Emily Apter describes translation as 'a petit métier, translators the literary proletariat'.[66] Since the (largely anglophone) apparatus of world literature depends entirely on the mechanism of translation, such a statement is surprising in its universal diagnosis of translators' lowly position within the literary system. The material contexts of literary translation show the limits of such a claim in the African literary space. British translators of

---

[65] Glover, 'Blackness', p. 30. [66] Apter, *Translation Zone*, p. xi.

African literature in the post-independence period were far from being a 'literary proletariat' without access to literary prestige or ownership of the means of production. In his critique of Apter, Venuti notes that 'the fact that humanistic translation still doesn't pay a subsistence wage in anglophone countries makes Apter's call for translators to "deown" their work not an "activist" strategy but sheer capitulation to exploitative copyright codes and publishing contracts'.[67] When we shift the perspective to material contexts of literary production in newly independent African nation states, access to copyright, fair pay, and (since the 1980s) the rapid professionalisation of literary translation in the anglophone global North (with expansion of university programmes, professional associations and bodies, and numerous workshops) become more lopsided still. The means of literary production, embedded in international copyright legislation established by the Berne Convention in the late nineteenth century, have meant that literary translators and publishers based in the global North often maintain ownership over publication rights for their translations.[68] This in turn stymies the possibility of publishing new translations of African literary texts by creating an imbroglio of rights issues that are only gradually being unpicked through groundbreaking collective efforts in recent years. The challenge of rene-gotiating rights falls to literary agents and publishing houses, as seen, for example, in the recent work of Éditions Flore Zoa; Raphaël Thierry at the Astier-Pécher Literary Agency; and the Alliance internationale des éditeurs indépendants.

Expatriate Translators and African University Life

Translators' archives are not only sources for tracing the translating process but also encourage reflection on archival volume and location and its potential distorting effects within world literary history. John Reed's uncatalogued archives were deposited in Chetham's Library, Manchester, UK, following his death in 2012.[69] They include 200

[67] Apter, *Against*, p. 319; Venuti, *Contra*, p. 70.
[68] See Roeschenthaler and Diawara, *Copyright Africa*.
[69] Reed and Wake also deposited papers at the University of Zambia in 1974 (Awung, 'Representing', p. 197).

volumes of diaries (kept daily from 1939 until 2012), 400 books, several boxes of correspondence, and a selection of journals, radical political pamphlets, and ephemera. These materials offer insight into expatriate university life and Southern African politics in this period, unfolding alongside Reed's work as an academic and literary translator and his interactions with African nationalist independence movements. Clive Wake's archives at the University of Kent include correspondence as well as numerous draft translation typescripts. Extensive correspondence with both translators is held in the archives of the Heinemann African Writers Series at the University of Reading. In what follows, the biographical detail and affect gleaned from the archive work to supplement existing critiques of the translations themselves by drawing attention to the lived experience of translating these texts. My reading signals the contingency of Reed's and Wake's labour, moving between Zimbabwe, Zambia (then Rhodesia and Nyasaland), and the UK as expatriate university lecturers. It also gleans absent voices and silences that resound in the archive and asks what role they played in projecting a literary commons within contexts of structural racism and embedded historical inequality.

Clive Wake was born in Cape Town in 1933, the son of a booking clerk on South African railways who wrote (unpublished) novels and stories attacking the racist status quo in South Africa. His mother worked as a school housekeeper after his father was killed during World War II. Wake studied French and English at the University of Cape Town, where he was taught by Dorothy Blair. He obtained a doctorate at the Sorbonne in Paris before taking up a teaching post at the University College of Rhodesia and Nyasaland (now University of Zimbabwe) in 1958, three years after that university received its Royal Charter which declared its non-racial admissions policy.[70] He left in 1966, moving to the University of Kent in the UK. It was while in Rhodesia that Wake met John Reed, living alongside him in the residence for unmarried staff members on campus. Reed was born in 1929 into a working-class family in Camberwell, South London. He gained a school scholarship, followed by a university scholarship to study English under C. S. Lewis at Magdalen College, Oxford. After military service, he

---

[70] Mackenzie, 'University of Rhodesia'.

taught in Edinburgh and at King's College London, and then took up a post to teach English at University College of Rhodesia and Nyasaland in 1957. A Labour Party supporter in Britain, while in Southern Africa, Reed became involved in African nationalist politics and trade union activism. He edited the journal *Dissent* with his colleague and Africanist historian Terence Ranger (1929–2015), who later took up the portentously named Rhodes Professorship of Race Relations at the University of Oxford. Among its coverage of Southern African nationalist politics, *Dissent* ran stories exposing the violent treatment of African detainees at Kanjedza detention camp in Nyasaland.[71] Reed's personal disquiet and refusal to settle in Southern Africa in this period emerge in his diaries. As he wrote in February 1964, 'my disgust with Britain doesn't help my determination to stay in Africa, because what I am really looking for is somewhere to live. Somewhere to belong, to settle – the baleful word. And obviously Africa can't satisfy this want.'[72] By 1965, following growing political tension in Southern Rhodesia and movement towards the Unilateral Declaration of Independence, Reed was forced to move to a post at the University of Lusaka in neighbouring independent Zambia, where he taught until 1974.

Tapiwa B. Zimudzi has written on the vetting, surveillance, and deportation of expatriate university lecturers in Rhodesia in this period. The crisis on campus included state surveillance of students and staff, with police allowed on campus.[73] There were violent discussions over academic freedom and integrity within the ostensibly cloistered space of the university as tensions emerged surrounding this 'new and daring experiment' of a multiracial institution in Southern Africa.[74] Such modes of state control were common amid dual fears of African nationalism and communism during the Cold War. Reed was issued an arrest warrant in 1965, and he

---

[71] On parallels between this camp and the treatment of Kenyan prisoners by British forces during the Mau Mau uprising, see McCracken, 'In the Shadow'.

[72] Diary entry, 29 February 1964, JR/C.

[73] This is documented in a report titled 'The Crisis in the University: An Account of the Events at the University College of Rhodesia and Nyasaland, March – April 1966', and in the mimeographed pages of *Dissent*. JR/C.

[74] Birley Report, JR/C.

documents the extensive surveillance of his colleagues in his diaries. While Wake was not so directly involved in radical student politics (working instead via the Catholic Church 'with great circumspection [. . .] in a much quieter way'),[75] racial politics shaped his experience of teaching French and translating from French in Rhodesia at this time. The status of other colonial languages within the curriculum at the time was not straightforward. There were no black African students of French at the university since French was not taught in segregated secondary schools for Africans at the time nor viewed as necessary for basic functional education. Wake describes a failed visit to see the Federal Minister of Education and request that French be added to the curriculum:

> He [the Minister] just turned it down flat; it's of no use to
> them – those were the attitudes in those days, racist atti-
> tudes; black people didn't need a full, broad education.
> Teach them English, teach them arithmetic, teach them
> some of the basics, and that's all they need.[76]

This approach was significantly more restrictive than extramural work happening in West and East Africa in the same period. Nonetheless, Wake was in regular contact with black students through his living arrangements as warden of the black students' residence. While African students were taught alongside white students in subjects such as history and English, they were segregated by race and gender in student halls. In the white female student residence, 'a whole corridor was set aside for the single black female student'.[77] The student's name was Sarah Chavunduka. The decision to move her into this residence was met with 'outrage' among many white students and their parents, serving as a stark reminder of the endemic racism and racial tensions in this university space.[78] There should be no overestimation of the radical influence of British academics in this period. Most African students already believed in the cause of African nationalism; they had no need for expatriate academics to 'convert them

---

[75] Interview, Clive Wake with Ruth Bush, 25 June 2019. [76] Ibid. [77] Ibid.
[78] Ranger, *Writing Revolt*, pp. 17–18.

to the cause'.[79] Similarly, there can be no equivalence made between the employment conditions faced by Reed and Wake and the structural racism faced by black students (and non-students) living in Rhodesia. Nonetheless, this lived experience on and off the university campus did contribute to the decision to undertake literary translations as a means of sharing literary voices from elsewhere on the continent – especially those voices perceived as racially empowering *and* aesthetically significant.

Informal pedagogical initiatives were an opportunity to introduce alternative literary voices. When students were arrested and taken to a detainment camp in 1959, Wake, Reed, and Ranger travelled there to teach. Wake also set up an African Night Schools Association in 1960, modelled on the one he had been involved in while living in Cape Town. Against this backdrop, translation served as a form of distraction: it 'took my mind off it'.[80] An amalgamation of diffidence and insistence on the value of translation characterises Wake's retrospective account of teaching and translating French. French had little vocational value, yet there was a powerful incentive to share literary voices emerging across the continent. The earliest readers for these translations were African students. As Wake notes retrospectively:

> I can't really teach any French to these black students, but I can make some contribution through translating African writers into English so that they can read them. And that was a very exciting thing for them. I can remember them saying on many occasions 'I would never have been able to read Senghor; I would never have been able to read Beti if you hadn't translated them'.[81]

'Distraction', 'Hackwork', or 'Drudgery'?

Translators' capacity to talk about their work in public and opportunities to do so have dramatically expanded over the past three decades. In global

[79] Zimudzi, 'Spies and Informers', p. 202.
[80] Interview, Clive Wake with Ruth Bush, 25 June 2019. [81] Ibid.

North settings, this correlates to the professionalisation of literary translation bodies and the growth of formal training and mentorship. For Reed and Wake, working long before this boom, translating began as a private leisure activity following their involvement in the 'Writing and Society in Africa' seminar convened by Terence Ranger at the university on 28–30 November 1958. Predating the famed 1962 Makerere Conference for African writers of English expression, this event brought together around fifty black and white lecturers, students, publishers (representatives of the Northern Rhodesia and Nyasaland Publications Bureau, and the Southern Rhodesia African Literature bureau), and journalists. The Shona writer and poet Solomon Mutsvairo spoke on 'Traditional uses of the vernacular' in Southern Africa and the list of participants includes future

Zimbabwe African National Union (ZANU) leader, poet, and liberation icon Herbert Chitepo. Wake and Reed delivered lectures on Negritude writing, Doris Lessing, and Alan Paton. It was a formative spark for Reed and Wake. Indeed, Wake admits having had no contact with African literature up to this point. His lectures evoke a burgeoning interest in Negritude and non-metropolitan writing in French. In this setting, the political and aesthetic project of Negritude chimed in tangential ways with local student-led nationalist politics. Reed's and Wake's dialogue with African students and embeddedness within university life shaped their choice of both *what* and *how* to translate, as well as the afterlives of their translations. This relationship between expatriate lecturers in anglophone African universities and the growth of African literature is a topic still requiring further research.[82] It raises fundamental questions concerning the role of formal educational institutions in the process of decolonisation, even as their curricula and staff body were very far from being 'decolonised' in the contemporary inflections of the term's reference to the project of pluriversal knowledge production.

---

[82] This research might consider how African nationalist movements responded to pedagogies aimed at cultivating academic values of detachment and objectivity derived from a complex Arnoldian legacy, alongside their commitment to recuperating endogenous knowledge systems. On extramural teaching in Ghana, see Skinner, 'Agency', p. 287.

Reed's diaries and fifty years of written correspondence with Wake situate their work within the messiness of everyday academic and personal life. Throughout the daily entries there are references to Reed's lingering, unfinished book on Edmund Spenser's *The Faerie Queene* (1590). The diaries give some sense of Reed's emotional difficulties and isolation as a gay man living in a highly conservative Rhodesian society. In October 1966, he mentions a love affair and considers stopping the diary at this point, for fear of being discovered. Many of the entries begin or end with concern over unmet deadlines, underprepared lectures, hangovers, depression, as well as politics.

> Very bad day. Sore from sunburn yesterday, tired, harassed
> by jobs to do, restless with sexual preoccupations – day
> spoilt with servant problems. Try to begin reading Petrarch,
> but make no progress. Life has lost meaning. What now?[83]

This particular diary entry's mention of 'servant problems' is as evocative as it is obscuring. Amid the many drinks parties, receptions, and dinners reported in the diaries, there is no mention of the people preparing these events or clearing away their aftermath.[84] Despite his later appreciation for Ferdinand Oyono's sensitive depiction of the servant protagonist Toundi in *Une vie de boy*, Reed's servants are not named in his diaries, nor discussed at any length.

Reed's role as a translator and reader of African literature was hesitant. He was a British academic trained in English textual criticism, committed to pursuing scholarship on early modern writing in English. Indeed, he queried in his diary whether he makes a 'turn to this African stuff since it is so difficult to make any progress with the Spenser away from the

---

[83]　Diary entry, 9 January 1961, JR/C.

[84]　In email correspondence with Felix Awung, Reed notes that he had not employed 'an African house servant' by the time he translated Oyono's novel but that he 'had plenty of opportunity to observe white management of kitchen staff' (Awung, 'Representing', p. 199).

libraries?'[85] This is African literary translation as distraction rather than activist mission. Reed was commissioned to translate *Une vie de boy* three years later. He writes again with a sense of hesitation:

> Perhaps this is hackwork not worth undertaking, but it might be useful if I want to get the chance to translate something later on to be able to say look, I did this book, you can get an idea from that . . . Also I am interested to see if I can do this translating of a novel really well.[86]

This entry indicates the relative value placed on literary translation in relation to that of literary criticism and scholarship (a hierarchy which has continued to resonate in many academic spheres).[87] 'Hackwork' is undertaken with reluctance on the basis of what it might lead to rather than for the prestige of translating Oyono's novel in the African Writers Series or its possible pedagogical uses as an incendiary anti-colonial classic. There is no mention of the novel's form or content.

By June that year, Reed writes: 'Slogging away at *Une Vie de Boy* as a kind of therapy. Drudgery but maybe exactly the drudgery I need at this moment. Nearly halfway.'[88] The task of this translator is expressed neither as a Benjaminian transcendental encounter with the 'pure language' nor as anti-colonial activism.[89] It is a calming activity, dulling and soothing personal difficulties and the political calamities, student detentions, bombs, and surveillance that characterised university life in Rhodesia and Nyasaland. In July 1964, Reed received comments on the translation from Clive Wake and describes his pleasure in revising the draft. He notes: 'I am shocked at how nervous I feel, how deeply I shall be vexed to read bad reviews. And this for a mere translation!'[90] The entry signals renewed pride and emotional investment in the work – and the culture of literary prestige at this time – despite a sense of its relative lack of merit. A vocabulary of modesty places translation in hierarchical relation to creative writing and (in Reed's case) literary

---

[85] Diary entry, 23 February 1961, JR/C. [86] Diary entry, 7 January 1964, JR/C.
[87] Harrison, 'World Literature'. [88] Diary entry, 11 June 1964, JR/C.
[89] Benjamin, 'Task of the Translator', p. 78. [90] Diary entry, 4 July 1964, JR/C.

criticism. This sits in counterpoint to the archived traces of their labour –
translating, editing translations collaboratively, consulting, and travelling –
which suggest Reed and Wake took the work very seriously. The diaries
remind us of the scale of Reed's and Wake's labour: largely dependent on
small networks of white expatriate academics and publishers, isolated encounters, and in Reed's case a muted translation imperative (at least in appear-
ances) rather than an explicitly political sense of mission.

This discussion does not aim to restore agency or prominence to Reed's
and Wake's work within the broader sweep of African literary history. It is
interesting to note that Heinemann invited Wake and Reed to include
photographs of themselves on the back cover of their anthology of
African poetry for the African Writers Series, in keeping with the series'
characteristic use of author photographs. Reed immediately declined and
cautioned against this since they were 'mere compilers'.[91] Archival microhistories enable a fuller account of African literary history, gesturing
through the strands of individual stories towards the power asymmetries
that obtain in that history.

Translating Negritude Poetry: Form, Language, and Materials

Wake's account of his career as a translator of African writers emphasises
a primary concern with form, especially in his translation of poetry, against
the backdrop of decolonisation. The primary aesthetic point of reference for
the early translations was the European literary canon, a canon in which
many of the writers were also steeped. In the proceedings from the 1958
Salisbury seminar, Wake comments on David Diop's 'Rama Kam' – an ode
to his first wife, the poet and journalist Virginie Camara:

> Unless the Western reader is prepared to abandon himself to
> the monotony of the poetic rhythms to be found in French
> West African poetry, he will find it simply tedious, whereas it
> really has an extraordinary fascination, mainly because of its
> insistence.[92]

---

[91] Letter from John Reed to Clive Wake, 17 January 1964, HEB 10/07/01, AWS/UR.
[92] 'Writing and Society in Africa', 1958, CW/P.

Wake foregrounds 'the' (implicitly homogeneous, though also gendered male) Western reader, while acknowledging a depth of insistent feeling grounded in poetic rhythm. This attempt to tune into the 'incantatory power' of the verse is rendered in bodily and spiritual terms, with a sense of curiosity, alongside the assertion of essential difference.[93] Wake and Reed maintain a circumspect approach to political aspects of African literature. Negritude poetry is 'in many respects artificial and probably transitory, but authentic and very rich', writes Wake in his 1958 paper.[94] He notes a 'tendency to identify culture with politics in a very narrow sense' and what he saw, at this time, as the revalorisation of a glorious African history masquerading as an 'extreme form of cultural nationalism'.[95] The primary emphasis on form is again found in Reed and Wake's translations of Senghor. These were undertaken initially as a leisure activity, and then published by Oxford University Press in 1965. Caroline Davis describes the tentative response of Oxford University Press to the proposal, which suggested that Senghor's poetry 'may be of interest and even a stimulus to English-speaking Africa, where the standard of poetry writing is so poor'.[96] Staff at Oxford University Press (based in the UK and Ghana) queried whether the poetry 'with a Laurentian message of black blood, could actually be harmful' in anglophone Africa.[97]

Despite Wake's and Reed's prolific output, literary translation was far from being lucrative. Literary translators have long been estranged from the circulation of prestige in literary and academic spaces. Prizes for literary translation emerged as a phenomenon only relatively recently. Reed notes in correspondence with Felix Awung that he was paid a lump sum of £100 for *Houseboy* and £150 for *The Old Man and the Medal*, and that all royalties then went 'very properly' to the author.[98] Reflecting on his translating career in 2019, Wake emphasises the number of copies sold and the fact that most sales were within Africa, rather than the advance and royalties

---

[93] Ibid. [94] Ibid.

[95] Ibid., p. 14. Gerald Moore criticises this aspect of Wake's reading of Negritude (Moore, 'African Writing', p. 88).

[96] Reed and Wake to Rex Collings, March 1962. Quoted in Davis, *Creating*, p. 111.

[97] Davis, *Creating*, pp. 112–13. [98] Awung, 'Representing', p. 204.

(2 per cent), which were shared between him and Reed. Royalties were 'absolutely trivial; you couldn't buy a coffee', though they continue to account for £100–£150 per year as a result of library photocopying legislation.[99]

The translatability of poetic form was an explicit factor in the selection of poems for Reed and Wake's 1972 anthology, *French African Verse*. Belletrism – that is, an approach to translating literature based on judgements of form and scant acknowledgement of the social contexts that shape literary judgements – has come under fire among some theorists and practitioners. Venuti's pointed critique of this approach among translators, editors, and workshop leaders argues instead for the development of a 'translation culture' with much greater awareness of social positioning and how it affects aesthetic judgement.[100] This line of argument claims that formalist approaches limit translators' ability to speak about their work and defend its value in meaningful ways (especially in contexts where translated literature is marginalised). In the case of Reed and Wake, translating for their students in Rhodesia, as well as for Oxford University Press's wider readership on the continent and in Britain, their aim was to introduce Negritude poetry *as poetry*. Such publications would simultaneously enable them to set these books for their teaching, though Reed also noted with respect to the second anthology, *A Book of African Verse*, that 'of course translations are not usually suitable for literary study'.[101] It remains something of a contradiction that there was little attempt to defend the ethical or political value of reading these translations as literary texts within Southern African classrooms. I will return to these ideas in Chapter 4, with reference to translation workshops in Cameroon, in order to reflect on the shifting

[99] Interview, Clive Wake with Ruth Bush, 25 June 2019.
[100] Venuti, *Translation*, pp. 247–8.
[101] Letter from John Reed to Clive Wake, 23 October 1962, HEB 10/07/01, AWS/UR. Wake commented facetiously to Reed regarding the anthology: 'We could then start prescribing our own books, which is the height of academic superiority. Perhaps we might then get some promotion!' (Clive Wake to John Reed, 8 October 1963, JR/C). No promotion was forthcoming (email correspondence, July 2021).

relationship between educational institutions, literary translation, and ideas of literary value.

Reed's and Wake's annotated poems, commentary, notes, and private correspondence provide a thick description of the translation process. This includes detailed discussion of vocabulary, poetic allusions, rhythm, style, sequences of tenses, punctuation, and the excess of articles in English. They do not claim authorial originality nor any exhaustivity in their approach. Indeed, their discussions are frequently marked by a sense of hesitation and a reading temporality which is contingent, partial, and provisional. Their introduction to *French African Verse* states:

> With Senghor we have not tried to match the assonance and alliteration of each line in our translation but to handle the long free-verse line in English so as to convey not only Senghor's meaning but the pomp and elaboration of his style. U'Tam'si is a difficult poet because of his obscurity and especially difficult to render into English because none of the literatures which use English have developed traditions of poetic surrealism. We have chosen poems and sections which seemed to offer the best chances of a satisfactory English version.[102]

This attention to what might be 'satisfactory' remains shaped by Wake's, and particularly Reed's, literary education, as well as an approach to translation based on formal equivalence. That the principle of selection is the poetry's translatability (rather than, say, potential legibility by a broad readership with different – perhaps incommensurable – cultural and literary reference points) confirms the power of the translators. In correspondence, Wake comments on Tchicaya U Tam'si's 'completely arbitrary and inconsistent' use of punctuation and capitals, suggesting that 'we can use our discretion and punctuate as we think fit'.[103] Co-translating was a drawn-out process which involved posting manuscripts between Salisbury (Harare)

---

[102] Reed and Wake, *French African Verse*, p. x.
[103] Letter from Clive Wake to John Reed, 6 April 1970, JR/C.

and London, ordering source books, and arranging trips to Paris to visit Présence Africaine and browse new titles. While Wake was steeped in French literary canon, he praised and sought out Reed's sense of 'English rhythms' as a vital contribution to the translation process.[104] Wake describes their collaboration:

> He [Reed] would always do the first draft, and then he'd send it to me and I would go through it, check the accuracy of the French translation, and make my own suggestions about perhaps changing the text a bit, and we'd send it backwards and forwards until we were satisfied.[105]

Wake's description refers consistently to ideas of 'accuracy' of linguistic content, with relatively little mention of cultural references. He also describes their attempt to generate equivalent effect:

> The rhythms of the language in English compared to French required you to do things. Sometimes we'd get a bit free with it. But our view was that translation was in a sense transposing, trying to convey in a form that is of literate English what the French-speaking writer was trying to do.[106]

In April 1961, Reed records in his diary that he is reading T. S. Eliot's translation of St John Perse's *Anabasis* as inspiration for his working translations of Senghor. As a reminder of the racial context, in the same entry, he records attendance of meetings of the Citizens against Colour Bar Association in Southern Rhodesia (a group convened by Terence Ranger which led direct action initiatives in the early 1960s). Correspondence with Senghor records the president's interest in these translations, which were among several English translations made of his work in this decade. Senghor's detailed edits of the translations are based on a critical rereading

---

[104] Letter from Clive Wake to John Reed, 26 January 1961, JR/C.
[105] Interview, Clive Wake with Ruth Bush, 25 June 2019. [106] Ibid.

by the professor of English at the recently inaugurated University of Dakar. During their Rockefeller-funded trip to Dakar in January 1962, Reed notes his hesitation: 'Horrified at first to read the translations. Yet force myself to face up to them, to resist the temptation to throw the whole lot, magnificently, out of the window.'[107]

From the late 1950s, Reed and Wake were exposed to debates concerning African languages and literary genres. Read more than six decades later, discussion of the 'language question' at the 1958 seminar is a salient reminder of how the teaching of literature and languages in universities has enacted – in unconscious and deliberate ways – forms of epistemic violence. Attendees debated African English literary style with reference to Tutuola's 'ungrammatical and idiosyncratic' language. They remarked on the dominant use of English at the university. The summary of the discussion notes:

> One ought to encourage the emergence of an English 'vernacular' as the common African literary language. Mr Reed agreed that variety was admirable so long as communication was made to other English speakers. He, the chairman [Terence Ranger] and Mr Brown commented on the difficulty of the academic instructor who had to compel a certain English style because it approximated to the intellectual attitude which underlay what were essentially European academic disciplines. This did not mean, as Professor McKenzie pointed out, that creative writing should be couched in this style. Creative writing was not, in fact, the responsibility or business of a university.[108]

University lecturers were aware of the colonial underpinnings of 'essentially European academic disciplines' and their embeddedness in 'a certain English style' of language. The simultaneous dismissal of creative writing in university settings, however, chimes with instrumentalist higher education

---

[107] Diary entry, 15 January 1962, JR/C.
[108] 'Writing and Society in Africa', 1958, CW/P, p. 36.

projects on the African continent in this period, where creative writing (and literary translation) had scant value as a form of knowledge production in and of itself on the official curriculum, despite flourishing literary production in student-led magazines.

In the subsequent discussion, participants debate the literary value of Zulu, Shona, and Ndebele, anticipating the themes that would dominate at Makerere in 1962 (and in its sizeable critical legacy). There was interest in learning and teaching French in Southern African schools, but 'not at the expense of the vernacular' which continued to be under threat due to 'missionary contempt for the vernaculars'.[109] The discussions signal a tension between the role and space of the university and the unpredictable agency of creative writing. While some expressed contempt for the future of 'vernacular' literature, Herbert Chitepo (the author of the epic Shona poem *Soko Risina Musoro*, published in a bilingual Shona–English edition by Oxford University Press that same year) commented on his relationship with the Shona language. He describes meeting with a rural elder while working as a teacher in 1944:

> He spoke Shona in a most wonderful way. Now what I intended to get from this was not to be able merely to reproduce the past that he had lived in. What I thought to get was inspiration in a way of expression, to hear his metaphors, the way he conveyed his thoughts, the juxtaposition of ideas, juxtaposition of visual images. I did not want to express the ideas he had, I wanted to express my own thoughts, but expressed through the pattern of speech the old man used; my own thoughts, but in a language enriched by a knowledge of the way in which my predecessors have expressed their ideas.[110]

Chitepo alludes to a process of creative writing and interpretation which goes beyond extractive logic based on content or recuperation of a pre-colonial past. He seeks to express meaning through the conscious use of form (the metaphors and juxtapositions) in order to render his own ideas in a reclaimed and recycled Shona. The colonial linguistic violence which

---

[109] Ibid, p. 44. [110] Ibid., p. 27.

necessitates such retrieval of an ancestral mode of expression – and its underpinning anti-colonial politics – can be glimpsed here.[111]

Chitepo's comment on travelling in order to gather literary and poetic materials provides a thought-provoking parallel to Wake and Reed's own travels together. It is a reminder of the kinds of mobility and research entailed in the labour of literary translation. Reed and Wake had access to ample material resources to support their work – symptomatic of both the wider global interest in African cultural production in the context of newly independent countries across the continent and Cold War soft power politics. In 1961, they were scouted by the Rockefeller Foundation for a grant to travel to West and Central Africa, Madagascar, Réunion, and Mauritius to conduct research, buy books, and meet writers. This funding lasted for the next four years, enabling them to curate a considerable collection of African literature at the university library, including Onitsha Market literature. They also spent time photocopying and gathering extensive primary material on the Madagascan poet Jean-Jacques Rabéarivelo while in Antananarivo. As Inderjeet Parmar has demonstrated, the Rockefeller Foundation sat alongside the Carnegie and CIA-sponsored Ford Foundations, amid American efforts to shape and manifest Cold War influence on the African continent.[112] Reed and Wake visited Senegal, Sierra Leone, Ghana, Nigeria, Benin, Cameroon, and Congo-Brazzaville during their first long trip in 1962. Wake recalls that they 'got the feel of these countries and the way people lived and worked' in ways which then informed their translations.[113] Reed's diaries provide a more underwhelming account of the trip. He mainly records illnesses and discomfort; there is no indication that Reed met with Ferdinand Oyono during this trip, though both he and Wake had helpful meetings with Senghor and consulted (anonymous) Wolof speakers while in Dakar to help with poetry

---

[111] Reed's later correspondence with editors at AWS about publishing books in local vernaculars (especially Shona), suggested that this would not be profitable and therefore better left to governments, missions, and local printers (Letter from John Reed to Keith Sambrook, 31 July 1964, HEB1 10/07/01, AWS/UR).

[112] Parmar, *Foundations*, pp. 169, 179.

[113] Interview, Clive Wake with Ruth Bush, 25 June 2019.

translations.[114] There is no recorded awareness of the contemporary political context in Cameroon, notably the French repression of the Union des Populations Camerounaises and the assassination of its leader, Ruben Um Nyobe. The ease of cross-continental mobility enabled in this period by foreign funding (for translators as well as for writers) created significant opportunities for literary encounters, agency, and resistance, enmeshed within the Cold War context. Reed and Wake's Rockefeller-sponsored journeys are a further demonstration of these transnational encounters. While signalling the perceived potential of European literary translators' labour in this period to challenge the reductive images of Africa, these grants suggest that funded mobility was a prized, yet partial and inevitably limited, mode of acquiring cultural and aesthetic knowledge.

Translators of African literary texts have historically operated within the dynamics of extroversion when selecting texts for translation and publication by Northern publishing houses and undertaking translation itself. Eileen Julien describes the anguish or sadness that accompanies liminality in the extroverted African novel (a novel 'that necessarily registers the imbalances of the world in which it arises', while remaining part of a much wider cultural ecology of popular print and oral forms).[115] Read against the backdrop of the last throes of colonial Rhodesia and the racial politics of Reed's (and Wake's) situated practice as a translator, texts including Oyono's novels gain further potency as a comment on interracial communication, power disparities, and the codes, etiquette, and conventions of colonial society. Senghor's poetry, read via the context of a racist university campus in Rhodesia and the work of liberal, expatriate university lecturers alongside African students, is disentangled from some of the debates concerning Negritude that have dominated critical discourse on his work. Recent discussions of Senghor's political and poetic work have recuperated the value of the latter in particular as an irruptive, liberatory, federating force.[116] Through translation, ideas of pan-African solidarity certainly travelled, but often in unanticipated and adaptive ways according to local contexts of reception. Further understanding of translators' lives informs

---

[114] Diary entry, 11 February 1965, JR/C. [115] Julien, 'The Extroverted', p. 696.
[116] Wilder, *Freedom Time*.

a more nuanced understanding of their work as literary mediators. Through these archival traces, we witness the messiness and affective dimensions of individual translators' lives – human qualities which tend to be submerged in structural and macro-level critiques of the global literary space.

Translation and Solidarity in the Black Atlantic

The remainder of this chapter asks how literary translation interacts with the materiality of print to conceal or actively display forms of violence. I centre the labour of a relatively unknown Cameroonian translator, Simon Mpondo, in the context of black Atlantic, pan-African politics. Mpondo's tragic life and poetry translations illuminate a shared horizon of the literary commons, despite clear disparities in translating strategy and social positioning. Unlike Reed and Wake, the few African translators of the so-called first generation of African literature have left little archival trace. As a result, scholarship has tended to focus on the more visible traces of white European translators. The translator's subjectivity is a central topic in postcolonial translation theory and practice. Retracing translators' lives reveals (while humanising, and thereby rendering more complex) structural inequalities in the access to apparatus of literary production and prestige. It also helps to map modes of literary activism that speak to Gould and Tahmasebian's four modes of 'translational activism': witness-bearer, voice-giver, vernacular mediator, and revolutionary.[117]

This case addresses the central issue – resurgent in the Gorman translator identity polemics – of who has the power to voice others and mediate for publication, and with what aesthetic consequences. Within the realm of professional literary translators (especially those located in the anglophone global North where translation accounts for a very small percentage of published books), many work part-time in precarious conditions with a commitment to the value of intercultural communication through literature. The undoing of these structural power disparities is gradual, simultaneously grappling with the dominance of English in the literary marketplace. Some critics argue for paratextual material that increases the reader's awareness of the text as a translation, though more common publishing practice effaces the translator

---

[117] Gould and Tahmasebian, *Routledge Handbook of Translation and Activism*, pp. 1–3.

in favour of the illusion of a transparent process of cultural transfer.[118] Others
have argued for providing additional contextual information when translating
African texts, while some assert the need for African translators for African
texts.[119] Following the previous sections' focus on the trajectories and aesthetic
strategies of Reed and Wake, I extend the argument in relation to discourses of
pan-African solidarity. Understood against the enduring signs of racial inequality that the renewed Black Lives Matter campaign has restored to headlines in
recent years, the following discussion asserts the need for historical nuance over
ideological polarity, while acknowledging that the scope for that nuance is often
missing from the archive and unobtainable through empirical research.

'Right On!' Simon Mpondo and the Translations of David Diop's Coups de pilon

The Heinemann archives reveal attempts to find anglophone African translators
for French texts. They also signal editorial attentiveness to the quality of
translations themselves, several of which had already been undertaken in the
United States.[120] The Cameroonian writer Mbella Sonne Dipoko, the Nigerian
film-maker Ola Balogun, and the critic Abiola Irele were all approached to
translate texts but did not take up the offer for logistical reasons of finances or
timings. Dipoko met James Currey in 1967 during the latter's visit to Paris,
where Dipoko was then living.[121] Following this, Dipoko, Irele, and Balogun
were offered the opportunity to translate Sembène's *Voltaïque* short story
collection. Currey also approached Dipoko for translations of Sembène's *Les
bouts de bois de Dieu* and Mongo Beti's *Le pauvre Christ de Bomba*. Given
Dipoko's lack of availability, Beti's novel was translated by Gerald Moore, who
noted that Dipoko 'probably needs the money more than I do and his knowledge of the Cameroons might be a strength in a translator'.[122] The American

---

[118] Batchelor, *Decolonizing*, p. 261.

[119] Appiah, 'Thick Translation'; D'Almeida, 'Literary Translation'.

[120] Bush, 'Publishing Francophone African Literature in Translation'.

[121] Interview, Ruth Bush with James Currey, 17 February 2011.

[122] Letter from Gerald Moore to James Currey, 8 May 1969, HEB 23/02, AWS/
       UR. Moore's manuscript was deposited at Université Yaoundé I, then Federal
       University of Cameroon, in 1973.

translation of Sembène's classic text was used, despite errors due to cultural illiteracy, for example repeated translation of the term 'brousse' as 'brush'.

Simon Mpondo was a Cameroonian national who co-translated David Diop's incendiary collection *Coups de pilon*, with Frank Jones, for Indiana University Press.[123] The details of his life are tragic and incomplete. Mpondo surfaces against the backdrop of transatlantic racial solidarity, as well as the necropolitical realities of Cameroon in the late 1970s which appear to have led to his violent death. While Reed and Wake depended on the structures of a robust postal service to work collaboratively over distance, the nature of Mpondo's working process with his co-translator and PhD supervisor, Professor Frank Jones, remains unclear.[124] Archives disguise and skew collective historical understanding, bringing a vivid image of one person to life while allowing another to fade entirely from the public record. My earlier reading of the 1958 seminar in relation to Reed's and Wake's trajectories is a case in point and invites a rereading of that event from the perspective of a specialist in Southern African and Shona literary history. The production of written history is laden with the power of archives to proffer apparent truths, compounded by issues of preservation and relative access to scholars from across the world. The question of the archive in African literary and cultural studies rightly continues to provoke debate concerning the politics of location, access, and curation.[125]

Poetry rewards retranslation. Its irruptive, allusive, and oral qualities invite multiple interpretations, while its formal attributes provide challenges beyond those of the realist novels which dominated African literature in the period of decolonisation. In deliberate contrast to the method adopted in the earlier sections of this chapter, I begin here by comparing the translated poems, before

---

[123] Steemers, *Francophone African*, pp. 70–1; p. 95n18.

[124] In the acknowledgements to his PhD thesis, Mpondo notes that Jones 'lent respectability to African literature by accepting to supervise the course in the department of Comparative Literature, and to jointly translate into English the poetry of David Diop' (p. 138).

[125] Ibironke, *Remapping*, pp. 32–5. For further recent debate, especially concerning the acquisition of African literary archives by American libraries, see Lindfors, 'Book Review Forum'.

considering the context of their translation and early reception. The aim is to highlight formal differences and suggest corresponding effects on interpretation. David Diop's poetic call to resistance, 'Défi à la force', is a helpful starting point:

'Defiance against Force',

John Reed and Clive Wake translation (*French African Verse*, Heinemann, 1972)

You, bowing, you, crying

You, dying, like that, one day without knowing why.

You, struggling, you watching over another's rest

You, looking no longer with laughter in your eyes

You, my brother, your face full of fear and suffering

      Stand up and shout NO!

'Challenge to Force', Simon Mpondo and Frank Jones translation (*Hammer Blows*, Indiana University Press, 1973)

You who bend you who weep

You who die one day just like that not knowing why

You who struggle and stay awake for the Other's rest

You with no more laughter in your look

You my brother with face of fear and anguish

      Rise and shout: NO!

Read in parallel and without recourse to Diop's French text, the differences in tenses, punctuation, lexis, and meter are manifold. Reed and Wake's more conventional use of commas and full stops delivers the poem as a series of visual and oral hesitations. A performance of this translation lends itself either to deliberate pauses emphasising the second-person address or to breathlessness caused by the irruptive caesurae, depending on the speed of reading. Meanwhile Mpondo and Jones invite a fluid articulation of the poem's call to resist. They leave the reader to find their own pauses: after the carefully poised 'rest' at the poem's midpoint or before each 'you', noticing the accumulation of second-person pronouns before the sudden acknowledgement of fraternal, racial solidarity – the ethical identification between poetic self and other (now singularised and gendered) – across the space from 'you' to 'my brother'. The capitalised 'Other's rest' contrasts with 'another's rest'. Rather than a case of 'arbitrary' typography as noted by Wake in relation to U Tam'si's verse, Mpondo and Jones invoke philosophical debates concerning the constitutive nature of Self and Other. While troubling a racialised hierarchical formulation of this relationship, it is not clear who this 'Other' is, nor why the addressee is watching them sleep. In the same line, Reed and Wake's 'watched over' invokes a scene of care with godlike and maternal resonances, though the phrasal verb 'stay awake for' points more to a more paranoid scene of protection from perceived threat (perhaps a fellow soldier).

Mpondo and Jones' choice of the relative pronoun 'who' and present tense throughout lends the poem a narrative shape with punctual, discrete events that accrue. Reed and Wake's opening verb, 'bowing', is more servile than Mpondo and Jones' choice, 'who bend'. The latter's translation culminates in the final 'rise and shout: NO!'. The spiritual dimension of 'rise' speaks to African American discourse of racial uplift, from the dense legacies of Du Bois and Booker T. Washington to subsequent articulations in Maya Angelou's *And Still I Rise* (published in 1978). The term also had wider potential significance to European contexts. The English-language translator of Frantz Fanon, Constance Farrington, originally proposed that *Les damnés de la terre* be titled *The Rising of the Damned*, making deliberate 'everyday' echoes of Italian and Irish uprisings (rather than the more obvious allusion to Charles Hope Kerr's English translation of the *Internationale*).[126] For Reed and Wake, the present participles provide a strong formal contrast in the final line's shift of tense: the resistant, secular, slightly prosaic, 'stand up' occurs grammatically in the midst of these repeated acts of crying, dying, and struggling rather than as a consequence of them or after they are complete (as might be implied in Mpondo and Jones' consistent use of the present tense). This close reading suggests possible interpretations of the two poems'

---

[126] Batchelor, 'Translation', pp. 48–9.

formal qualities in the English chosen by their translators. Rather than measuring their success against normative aesthetic criteria of value, it signals how small differences in translators' choices affect this poem's direct call to reject the violent colonial status quo. To compare now to Diop's French text:

'Défi à la force', David Diop (*Coups de pilon*, Présence Africaine, [1956] 1973).

Toi qui plies toi qui pleures
Toi qui meurs un jour comme ça sans savoir pourquoi
Toi qui luttes qui veilles pour le repos de l'Autre
Toi qui ne regardes plus avec le rire dans les yeux
Toi mon frère au visage de peur et d'angoisse
                    Relève-toi et crie: NON!

Diop's poem shares the syntactic approach of Mpondo and Jones. Its irregular line lengths and lack of punctuation (a consistent feature of Diop's *oeuvre*) are given coherence through the anaphoric 'Toi qui', where the informal second-person pronoun immediately establishes a relationship between the poetic voice and the addressee. The rhymed 'pleures'/'meurs' link the human, emotional expression of abjection to complete bodily collapse. There is sad irony in the 'sans savoir pourquoi' given this poem's exposition of structural oppression. The poem raises the question of readerly address in particularly insistent and apposite ways. The addressee of the poem is too crushed and exhausted to recognise the cause of his own oppression, leaving space for the poetic voice to declare a shared imperative of resistance, and perform the power of such a dialogic invocation.

   Wake and Reed were keen to undertake the translation of the whole of *Coups de pilon*. However, the existence of the Indiana University Press edition by Mpondo and Jones precluded this, as recorded in Wake's reader's report and correspondence between Reed and Wake.[127] Wake noted that the poetry 'had been well translated' and commented on Mpondo's accompanying essay, 'which conveyed very well the emotional appeal Diop has for Africans and

---

[127] Letter from John Reed to Clive Wake, 25 March 1973, CW/P.

which we would have talked about; here it is demonstrated. It's disappointing, but on the other hand heartening to have an African name on the title page.'[128] In his report on the translation for Heinemann, Wake notes that the essay 'has a polemic edge to it which tends to distort and get in the way of the author's literary judgement at times; he is quite obviously emotionally involved in what he is writing.'[129] This affective dimension is further revealed if we turn to the transatlantic context in which Mpondo was working.

Mpondo travelled to the University of Washington in Seattle to undertake his PhD in the late 1960s, which he completed in 1971 under the title 'From Independence to Freedom: A Study of the Political Thinking of Negro-African Writers in the 1960s'.[130] He had previously studied Political Science at Tufts University in Boston, and completed an MA in Comparative Literature from City College of New York. He published an article about David Diop in *Présence Africaine* in 1970 which was later expanded as the accompanying essay in the American edition of *Hammer Blows* (the Heinemann African Writers Series edition did not include this essay, for reasons of budget and perceived relevance). In 1973, he took up a post at Stockton University in New Jersey before returning to Cameroon in 1974 with his American wife. They had two sons and Mpondo, now an established *cadre*, taught at the Federal University of Cameroon. He wrote poetry (his 'The Season of Rains' appears in the *Penguin Book of Modern African Poetry*) and took up a role with an oil company following the growth of Cameroon's oil production in 1977. Mpondo was living in Douala when he and his family were killed by strangulation in 1979. The 'affaire Mpondo' is a shadowy event in this period of Ahmadou Ahidjo's presidency in Cameroon (a presidency, as Achille Mbembe has argued, marked by forms of *commandement* and violent excess).[131] One source suggests that this was the result of a lack of political cooperation over oil company files, highlighting the difficult adjustment of

---

[128] Letter from Clive Wake to John Reed, 22 June 1973, CW/P.

[129] Report on translation of *Coups de Pilon*, from Clive Wake to James Currey, 6 May 1973, HEB 03/02, AWS/UR.

[130] Thanks to Susan R. Henderson (a former student of Mpondo) and librarians at Syracuse University for making the microfilm of this dissertation available as a PDF.

[131] Mbembe, *On the Postcolony*.

Ahidjo's government to the new oil economy.[132] Two of Simon Mpondo's brothers died subsequently in unexplained circumstances: Robert Mpondo (a lecturer at the University of Ngaoundéré, killed in Douala in 2002) and Armand Mpondo (who died in Paris after a suspicious car accident). Christian Mpondo, a former militant with the opposition Union des Populations du Cameroun (UPC) Party, publicly expressed fears regarding the persecution of his family in a newspaper article published in 2006.[133] The 'affaire Mpondo' remains a murky reminder of the necropolitics which have shaped six decades of autocratic political rule in Cameroon. Viewed alongside Mpondo's work as a translator of David Diop, this incomplete reminder of violent physical erasure and corresponding archival absence acts as recuperation, however limited, of his labour within the African literary space and reignites the spark of Diop's poetry of resistance. His former colleagues at Stockton University, the poet Thomas Kinsella and his colleague Ken Tompkins, write movingly of Mpondo: 'his loss is much more than a tiny statistic hardly remembered by anyone. He was here on this campus, in some of these classrooms teaching students very much like all of us. In a strange way, he was us.'[134]

The paratexts of Mpondo's translations, alongside the translations themselves, offer the most obvious parallel insight into his approach as a translator and literary critic. Mpondo's essay on David Diop, included in the American edition only, signals his interest in the radical, Marxist dimensions of Negritude. He defends Diop against Senghor's 'attempt to straitjacket' him in the prefatory note to Diop's poems in the landmark 1948 *Anthologie de la nouvelle poésie nègre et malgache*. Mpondo paraphrases Frantz Fanon's suggestion that the poet must display 'a constant concern with specifying the historic moment of the struggle,

[132] Mbangue Nkomba, 'Pétrole', n.p., section 2, paragraph 1. On the connection between Cameroon's oil extraction (including its deepening of the 'fêlure' between francophone populations and marginalised anglophone populations who lived principally in oil-extracting regions) and the widening socio-economic wealth gaps within the country, to the benefit of its political elite, see Deltombe, Domergue, and Tatsitsa, *Kamerun!*, pp. 637–40.
[133] Fouda, 'Ces martyrs'; Mba Talla, 'Cameroun'; Pene, 'Christian'. The precise details of this history remain difficult to access.
[134] Tompkins and Kinsella, 'Simon Mpondo'.

with limiting the field in which action will unfold, the ideas around which the popular will is to crystallize'.[135] This emphasis on guiding 'the popular will' chimes with Mpondo's use of the radio in the United States, as well as his readings in prisons. For Mpondo, Diop's use of optimism, humour, and irony avoided his poetry becoming 'anesthetized by too much academic training', unlike that of Senghor. Diop 'constantly lets his imagination play over and integrate itself into the scene he is describing'.[136] In his reading of 'Rama Kam' – Diop's sensual ode to his first wife, Virginie Camara – Mpondo argues that 'it is Diop who sounds like an activist, with a pen dipped in his own red blood'. The critical language is far removed from that of Reed and Wake's formalist reading as they began to encounter African literature in the late 1950s in their respective interpretive community in colonial Rhodesia.

Mpondo connected Diop's writing to struggles for freedom on both sides of the Atlantic. In his translation of 'Nègre clochard', the poem Diop dedicated to Aimé Césaire, Mpondo notes that the poet 'seems to have foreseen the debacles that were to mark the post-independence era when rulers crushed every latent opposition':

'Nègre clochard' (*Coups de pilon*, Présence Africaine, 1973 [1956]).

. . .

Patience le Carnaval est mort
J'aiguise l'ouragan pour les sillons futurs
Pour toi nous referons Ghâna et Tombouctou
Et les guitares peuplées de galops frénétiques
A grands coups de pilons sonores
De pilons
Eclatant
De case en case
Dans l'azur pressenti.

---

[135] Mpondo, 'Assessing', pp. 69–70. [136] Ibid., pp. 71–2.

'Negro Tramp', Mpondo and Jones translation (*Hammer Blows*, Indiana
   University Press, 1973)

. . .

Patience the Carnival is dead
I whet the hurricane for future furrows
For you we will remake Ghana and Timbuktu
And guitars peopled with frantic gallops
To the sound of mighty pestle blows
Pestles
Bursting
From hut to hut
In the foreknown azure.

These closing lines assert a cacophony of resistance contrasting with the
previous sections' portrayal of dehumanisation and submission: a whetting
stone, guitars, frenetic hooves, pestles pounding, which then quieten to the final
release of 'l'azur pressenti'. French symbolists, whose poetry Diop had studied,
used the intense and rare blue found in lapis lazuli to denote spiritual and
transcendental values with 'seductive agency'.[137] For Stéphane Mallarmé, azure
(the title of his first major poem) 'visualizes the ideal space of fuller, deeper
poetic consciousness; but its mocking agency invariably checks that aspiration
and affirms its susceptibility to being traduced.'[138] Diop's poem finds resonance
here, where azure is 'at once evidence of hue and intimation of heaven' but in
tension with disillusionment.[139] The violence of the aural and visual qualities
that characterise Diop's homage to Césaire invokes the hue of the cloudless sky
(an anticipated realm of hope, possibility, and freedom). It also evokes an
allusion to a sea which is already *felt* or *known* somehow following a scene of
battle and pillage. The spectral wake of the middle passage is present alongside
the ethereal and anticipated sense of release through this colour concept.

   Mpondo and Jones maintain the allusion to women's labour within this
poem's scenes of conflict through the 'sound of mighty pestle blows'. It is

[137] Harrow, *Colourworks*, p. 49. [138] Ibid., p. 53. [139] Ibid., pp. 52–4.

interesting to note, therefore, the decision to translate the title of the anthology (*Coups de pilon* in French) as *Hammer Blows* (apparently a suggestion of the Présence Africaine editor, Mr H. Jones, rather than the translators) which erases the gendered implication of 'pestle blows' used in the context of this poem. As found throughout francophone African literature of this period, the rhythm of food being pounded by women using the pestle and mortar conveys a soothing sonic and visual landscape. To give just one memorable example from the same period, Ousmane Sembène's *Les bouts de bois de Dieu*:

> Avant même que l'étoile du matin eût disparu dans les premières lueurs de l'aube, commençait le chant des pilons. De cour en cour, les pileuses se renvoyaient le bruit léger du martèlement incessant de leurs pilons et ces bruits semblaient cascader dans l'air bleuté comme le fait le chant des ruisseaux [. . .] Le vieux mortier de la cour avait été un arbre; ses racines plongeaient encore dans la terre.[140]

Sembène's description conveys the sounds of dawn food preparation in idealised harmony and communal connection. The pastoral lyricism of the simile connects the sounds of the pestle hitting the mortar to the natural world, further emphasised with the acknowledgement that the material of the mortar itself was once a deep-rooted tree. Despite his reputation as a social realist writer, Marxist-Leninist, proto-feminist critic of Senghorian Negritude, this passage resounds with the poetic association of women with the African land mass familiar in Negritude writing. The decision to translate Diop's anthology as *Hammer Blows* draws on a different image of labour, evoking political associations with the industrial, urban, working-class, and

[140] Sembène, 'Les bouts' p. 158. 'In the old days, the singing of the pestles had begun even before the morning star disappeared in the first light of dawn. From courtyard to courtyard the women had exchanged their unceasing, pounding rhythms, and the sounds had seemed to cascade through the smoky air like the song of a brook rushing through a deep ravine [. . .] The old mortar in Niakoro's courtyard had been a tree; its roots were still sunk deep in the earth' (Sembène, 'Gods Bits', pp. 97–8).

international socialism. Such paratextual decisions by publishers work to marginalise the foregrounding of women's presence in the poetic texture not only as objects of desire commonly found in Diop's poetry ('Rama Kam', 'To a Black Dancer') and maternal care ('A ma mère') but as social actors.

Diop's poems, Mpondo notes, 'sparkle with hot, beautiful impudences', attacking colonialism and oppression across geographies.[141] Their intertextual resonances are characteristic of poetic left Pan-Africanism as a 'poetry of ideas'.[142] Aural qualities in the poems made them excellent candidates for public readings. In a fascinating and rare record of reader responses, Mpondo notes:

> The present writer recalls readings before audiences in various corners of the North American continent, and was most impressed by the visceral response forthcoming in the Washington State Reformatory at Monroe near Seattle, Washington. He was constantly interrupted by exclamations such as 'Right on!' 'Yea!' 'Tell 'em!', and by many other much less reproducible groans of total approval. Those prisoners, who were all black, perceived and visualized a condition which David Diop had expressed, a contradiction between the heroic ancestral past and the ignominious colonial present. Diop, who always managed to transcend the here and now for the benefit of the universal and the eternal, projected the resolution of that contradiction into a future age of freedom for all. No wonder prisoners, who lived on hope, cheered so loudly.[143]

This prison education programme provided a new context for Diop's radical poetic vision via the voice and bodily presence of his Cameroonian translator. Such glimpses of the poems circulating before new audiences in the United States in the heady civil rights period of the early 1970s evoke an irretrievable archive of readerly responses. This is 'page poetry' becoming 'stage poetry'.[144] Elsewhere, Mpondo describes

---

[141] Mpondo, 'Assessing', p. 75.
[142] Okewole, cited in Suhr-Sytsma, 'Theories', p. 592. [143] Ibid., pp. 77–8.
[144] Jaji, 'Our Readers', p. 71.

how another poem, 'Le temps du martyr', 'has become a favorite battle hymn of pan-Negrism. It gives pleasure to blacks in Harlem and Sophiatown, in Kingston and Duala [*sic*]. Diop's imagination could not have received a better tribute'.[145] This poem sets out with economical diction the hypocrisy and dehumanising racism of white supremacy.[146] Once again, Mpondo alludes to the poetry's reception in English translation as a 'vehicle of Third World culture', circulating at multiple overlapping scales and forging simultaneous forms of solidarity and pleasure. While in the United States, Mpondo hosted a radio show entitled 'African Times' from January to August 1970 on the Seattle-based station KRAB. The programme featured 'an emphasis on African literature and culture, with an occasional discussion of current African events'.[147] In an article for *Présence Africaine*, Ruth Simmons mentions the powerful reception of Diop's poetry among young African Americans, from his poems on African femininity to those on specifically American themes (the lynching of Emmett Till in 1955 following his alleged whistling at a white woman), and the need for a full English translation. His voice, she writes, 'is that of an African poet pleading for his people's cause and who dedicates himself not to the icy kingdom of pure poetry, but to the volcanic region which is life'.[148] Mpondo's brief sketch of his reading public is painfully poignant in the present moment of mass incarceration of Black people in the United States. It re-exposes the gulf between the utopian promise of Diop's poetic call for freedom and the lived structural conditions of politically sanctioned state violence. It also signals a moment – however fleeting – and an affirmation of shared affective experience in the poetic performance.

Without archival density, this microhistory of Simon Mpondo positions his life and translations of *Coups de pilon* against a backdrop of global

---

[145] Mpondo, 'Assessing', p. 85.

[146] For a fascinating comparative discussion of three English translations of this poem, see Yesufu, 'A Note', pp. 309–10.

[147] Thanks to Charles Reinsch from KRAB archive for providing details of these programmes and confirming that recordings have not survived (email correspondence).

[148] Simmons, 'La pertinence', p. 92. My translation.

racialised oppression, as well as that of postcolonial violence within Cameroon. It pitches a counterargument to the a priori value of archival methodologies, with a reminder of the intersecting value of close textual analysis (my own, but in particular brief insights from contemporary testimonies and subsequent reader responses). Mpondo's work as an activist translator – on the radio, in prisons, and in universities – cannot be disentangled from the transatlantic circuits of Third Worldist solidarity evoked in his essay and in Diop's own poetry. It resounds within his translations and in the brief glimpses of their reception. Informed by ideas of racial solidarity, his translation and sharing of African literature also involved negotiating and exposing moments of incommensurability and difference. One of his former students recalls Mpondo's direct rebuke to a Black American student in his Seattle classroom who equated American racialised experience with that of Africans: 'Instead of what one would expect from a sympathetic professor in those days, he said something on the order of the student having no idea about the situation in Africa [. . .] Africa did not equal America [. . .] it made us all sit up – what did we not know?'[149] In contrast to but not entirely distinct from Reed and Wake, I have foregrounded the nature of Mpondo's translating subjectivity and the evocation of the translator as one of an engaged figure of resistance. Mpondo's translation imperatives are grounded in post-independence pan-African ideals to inspire informed solidarity and resistance at multiple levels. The elusive history of his later life and death points to the difficulty of grasping the lived realities of that resistance in Cameroon during the late 1970s.

The visibility and activist imperative of translators' labour are integral to the wider ecology of African literature and can inform new readings, as these examples demonstrate. Translators' location in the literary field and social positioning (through gender, race, sexuality, geographical location, education trajectory, and social class) inform their translating strategies at the level of form and paratext, including affecting how the text is read. As will be explored in Chapter 4 of this book, the relationship to readers is central to current initiatives to translate and retranslate African writing. That relationship shifts within structural contexts of a literary marketplace which is fractured, dispersed, and rarely 'global' in any meaningful material

---

[149] Susan R. Henderson, email correspondence, 23 June 2021.

sense. Book distribution remains a perennial issue, as does the economic weight of minority-world publishers in the global North, yet a number of initiatives driven by literary collectives based on the African continent are undertaking the work of editing, publishing, and giving visibility to new writing. In parallel, literary translation continues to take place beyond the consecrated space of print publication, in school and university classrooms, in workshops, in missionary-led language initiatives, and in private homes. At a time when there is renewed interest in the theorisation of poetry in relation to ideas of race and social connectivity, attention to literary translation and literary translators offers an important avenue for reflection on African writing as 'praxis-based theorising'.[150] Evincing the limits of a theory/practice distinction, the role of translators within diasporic publishing initiatives and long-standing literary magazine culture on the African continent, alongside more recent literary activist networks, is decisive in the multilingual, world-making dynamics of African literature. It is with an eye to the multiple, often ephemeral, dimensions of translation and its empowering, 'volcanic' potential,[151] despite oppressive structural conditions, that the final part of this study seeks to explore the current renaissance in African literary translation.

[150] Suhr-Sytsma, 'Theories', pp. 585–6. [151] Simmons, 'La pertinence', p. 92.

4 Translation Workshops: Multilingualism and Epistemic Violence in Contemporary Cameroon

It is an excellent thing to blend different worlds; whatever its own particular genius may be, a civilization that withdraws into itself atrophies; that for civilizations, exchange is oxygen [. . .] But then I ask the following question: has colonization really *placed civilizations in contact*? Or, if you prefer, of all the ways of *establishing contact*, was it the best? I answer no.[152]

Aimé Césaire's elemental metaphor for transcultural encounters speaks to the recurring motif of shared air and breath within the commons. While John Reed struggled to breathe in the stifling temperatures during a Rockefeller-funded tour of West Africa, asphyxiation occurred in the violent murder of Simon Mpondo's family in post-independence Cameroon. In more recent times, Carli Coetzee has spoken and written of the need for academic practice to move 'outside the air-conditioned room' of conference centres and well-endowed universities in the global North, to create corridors 'where there is a mingling of the air, and the humidity and atmosphere, of different environments'.[153] Meanwhile, the global pandemic of an airborne coronavirus and the murder by asphyxiation of George Floyd have rendered mutual dependencies, vulnerabilities, and historical and structural violence in stark relief. In this context, what role might remain for the labour of translation within the discourses of globalisation, mobility, cultural encounter, and world literature which depend on the term as a metaphorical anchor? How does this question play out differently across contrasting scales and material contexts? How do literary form and language, as well as practical initiatives, generate responses to these questions, via differently sited readerships? Where Kaima Glover speaks of the 'high-stakes' work of translating Haitian literature for an Afro-diasporic readership, this chapter considers the views of contemporary translators based on the African continent who translate with a local readership foremost in

---

[152] Césaire, *Discourse*, p. 33. [153] Coetzee, 'Unsettling', p. 106.

mind.[154] Its particular focus is on the 'unique position' of anglophone Cameroon – a culturally marginalised space with deep significance for thinking through the politics of language.[155] I set out to illustrate how literary translation operates as a practical and ethical imperative in contemporary Cameroon. Via discussion of the practical experience of scoping and co-organising the Bakwa literary translation workshop in Yaoundé in 2019, I document a translation project that did not centre either unconsciously or via its publishing trajectory on a projected readership located in the global North. The analysis addresses a significant gap in critical literature surrounding pedagogy in literary translation workshops, while contributing to methodological debates in African, comparative, and world literary criticism.

Reflection on the role of workshops (both creative writing and translation) in Cameroon expands ideas of what literature is and does in contexts of protracted conflict (namely the Anglophone Crisis which has rocked the country since 2016). I argue that contrasting contemporary translation imperatives in this space propose theories in practice which make visible the material dimensions and historically embedded forms of epistemic violence. The arguments disturb universalising tendencies of Translation Studies as an academic discipline and pose new avenues of reflection for a professionalised literary translation workshop circuit primarily situated in the anglophone global North. This case study also challenges reductive understandings of 'global anglophone' hegemony by discussing a space where the anglophone minority population is subject to forms of domination by the state and there is an active and historical armed separatist movement along linguistic lines. A more nuanced form of multilingual, mixed methodology embedded in material realities of (re)translation and attuned to the situated, pragmatic optimism of the current generation of literary producers is proposed as an alternative path ahead.

[154] Glover, 'Blackness', p. 30. For further discussion of translation and Blackness in American contexts, see Keene, 'Translating Poetry'; Coleman, 'Publishers'.

[155] Ashuntantang, 'Publishing and Dissemination', p. 246. See also Nfah-Abbenyi and Doha, 'Fragmented Nation'.

This chapter's methods engage in critical listening to some of the conversations, frictions, and compromises that emerge from present-day translation imperatives in the transnational, multilingual contexts of contemporary Cameroon. After an opening overview of counter-hegemonic moves in the contemporary African literary space and contextualisation of Cameroonian multilingualism, I draw on ethnographic tools in fieldwork (interviews, observation, focus groups) and participatory action research methods to discuss the 2019 Bakwa workshop. I do so with a critical eye to the colonial legacies of ethnography and its potential to reify subject/object positions, as well as the proven potential of such methods to produce useful forms of knowledge and understanding within African literary studies.[156] Space is given to the voices of those who took part in the workshop, alongside acknowledgement of how Western funding continues to support such ventures in ways which are frequently contested.[157] There is no straightforwardly 'pure', 'autonomous' alternative proposed within the so-called hustle of African letters.[158] I emphasise furthermore, via readings of Bakwa's publications and texts translated during the workshop, the necessity of attending to what Peter D. McDonald terms the 'generative potential' of literary writing itself, alongside sociological and materialist approaches to literature and translation.[159] This discussion of literary translation workshops elucidates some of the book's preceding arguments regarding multilingualism and coloniality in the literary commons by

---

[156] See Cahill et al., 'Participatory Ethics'. For further examples of fieldwork and participatory methods within African literary studies, see Kiguru, 'Language and Prizes'. On the meeting points between the humanities, postcolonial studies, and social scientific methods, see Ducournau's sociological study of the making of 'African classics' (*La fabrique*); Wells et al., 'Ethnography'; Go, *Postcolonial Thought*, pp. 187–9.

[157] My thanks to workshop organisers and participants Dzekashu MacViban, Mariette Tchamda Mbunpi, Ray Ndébi, Ros Schwartz, Edwige Dro, Madhu Krishnan, and Georgina Collins for their encouraging comments on this chapter.

[158] Ngũgĩ and Murphy, 'African Literary Hustle'; Krishnan, *Contingent*, pp. 67–9.

[159] McDonald, 'On Method', p. 308.

drawing together future-oriented threads concerning digital technology, pedagogy, and retranslation.

Materiality, Form, and Translation in the Contemporary African Literary Scene

While aiming to ensure fair payment and equitable distribution, publishing infrastructure surrounding African literature has remained a zone of capitalist control and – at times – exploitation. Publishing contracts have historically repeated an extractive gesture by agents located in the global North, despite the forms of political solidarity to be found when delving into individual cases such as that of Simon Mpondo, Frank Jones, John Reed, and Clive Wake. This situation is changing rapidly and remains an important topic for current and future research. During a panel on the topic of literary translation at the 2020 Aké Festival of Arts and Books – the continent's largest literary festival, now based in Lagos – the novelists Khadi Hane and Hemley Boum and the literary agent and scholar Raphaël Thierry discussed the role of the author in negotiating distribution and translation rights for their work on the continent.[160] They stressed local-level interventions at each link in the book production and distribution process, as well as the key role of Africa-based publishing houses, sometimes working through support networks of the African Books Collective and the Alliance internationale des éditeurs indépendants. In Cameroon, Boum's novels are distributed by the Grand Vide Grenier group, a local start-up founded in 2013 which provides an online book order and delivery service that does not require a debit or credit card, unlike other major global online book vendors.[161] This start-up makes books available through local outlets, including petrol stations and supermarkets, though it has also faced criticism for the additional delivery costs incurred. Khadi Hane, whose first books were published by Nouvelles Éditions Africaines in Senegal, described how her books are published in France, with a specific contractual clause on 'non-exclusive rights' enabling African editions. This has led to

---

[160] Blédou et al., 'A propos'.
[161] They are also available in the Peuples noirs, Peuples africains bookshop, founded by Mongo Béti.

the recent new edition of her novel *Des fourmis dans la bouche*, co-published by eight Africa-based publishing houses as part of the *Terres solidaires* collection. This collection has existed since 2006 and published authors including Véronique Tadjo, Ken Saro-Wiwa, Léonora Miana, and Djaïli Amadou Amal. Prices are kept accessible, between 2,500 and 3,500 CFA (around 5 euros), for a wide readership located on the continent. These books are given a 'livre équitable' ('fair book') badge by the Alliance internationale des éditeurs indépendants, signalling their adherence to a model of publishing based on solidarity, economies of scale, exchange of best practice, and acknowledgement of local contingencies, including standardising book prices. Such initiatives, working at a granular local scale while using international funding (*Terres solidaires* is funded by the Organisation internationale de la Francophonie), are symptomatic of how some literary producers navigate a legal apparatus and distribution infrastructure that offers both challenges and opportunities for African writers, translators, and publishers in the twenty-first century.[162]

Initiatives to support and sustain literary translation as a feasible activity on the African continent continue to grow as part of wider efforts to build sustainable literary infrastructure. These initiatives include literary prizes; multilingual publications blending digital print and audio files (the *Valentine's Anthology*, published by Cassava Republic's Ankara imprint; *Jalada*'s translation issue); Boubacar Boris Diop's Ceytu series of francophone classics in Wolof translation; the Cape Town–based multimedia project, *Chimurenga*; and the work of *Bakwa* magazine and their publishing arm Bakwa Books in Cameroon. Continuing a long tradition of small magazine publishing on the African continent, Bakwa is a digital platform for avant-garde creative writing and cultural criticism. Founded in 2011 by Dzekashu MacViban, it has to date existed as a magazine

---

[162] A further example is Éditions Flore Zoa, a Swiss publishing house that specialises in African writing (in French and in French translation) and aims to republish classic African texts published outside the continent making them available to Africa-based readers. In 2021, they acquired rights for works by Ferdinand Oyono, Cheikh Hamidou Kane, and Boubacar Boris Diop, after publishing a French translation of Ayobami Adébayo's bestselling *Stay with Me*.

(available in PDF and print), digital web platform, and podcast with a robust social media strategy on Twitter, Facebook, Instagram, and YouTube. In 2019, it launched its print-publishing initiative. Bakwa is primarily anglophone, but includes pidgin, hispanophone, and francophone content. It has built collaborations with the Mexico-based online magazine *Ofi Press*, California-based Phoneme Media, and Nigeria-based *Saraba* magazine. Bakwa's ethos is internationalist and pan-African. As part of a constellation of avant-garde digital publishing on the African continent, it contributes to a counter-hegemonic movement within the global literary field, blending written, oral, and visual material, and foregrounding translation. What these platforms share is a self-conferred 'activist' ethos committed to building a literary infrastructure capable of bypassing Western publishing houses and media platforms. They exist in plural forms, encouraging new writing through the organisation of and participation in literary festivals, events, workshops, and literary prizes on the continent.[163] The public sphere surrounding these initiatives is increasingly acute in tone, creating a buzz around African literature which is 'a space for contention and debate rather than only celebration and support'.[164] Despite inequalities in internet access across the African continent and their small scale, these initiatives 'expand the notion of the literary and cultivate[s] networks of friendship and intimacy towards a new way of experiencing and thinking the world'.[165] Such affective dimensions of the literary commons manifest in both the material contexts and the transnational literary content of Bakwa.

The magazine includes several creative meditations on multilingualism as a political issue and as affective, embodied experience. To give just one example of the agency or 'generative potential' of this literary content,[166] *Bakwa 8*'s 'Pain' issue, features a short story by the South African writer Isabelle Morris. Morris' story 'How to Learn a Language' dissects the emotional suffering of a widow, Kamila, who struggles with grief. The story thematises language learning, editing, and pedagogy as therapeutic exercises for grief and its inexpressivity. Kamila is hospitalised following a mental breakdown after the death of her husband. Her fragile emotional

---

[163] Nesbitt-Ahmed, 'Reclaiming'. [164] Jaji, 'Our Readers', p. 84.
[165] Krishnan, *Contingent*, p. 83. [166] McDonald, 'On Method', p. 308.

state is described through her attempts to learn English and the lessons set by her teacher, through which she channels her feelings into English-language exercises. In one of these, she is asked to write a short text in fifty words. These exercises appear in print with certain words crossed out. The text's authority and implied authorship remain suspended as it is unclear whether this gesture is self-correction or correction by her teacher:

> When the mobile phone battery ~~dead~~ died and her charger would not work, Kamila became hysterical. The doctor gave her an injection in her bottom, right through her stiff, new nightdress. 'It will not ~~go on forever~~ continue, she will ~~forget~~ get better,' he said.

The language of memory, death, and time is highlighted through its erasure in the typography. The technology of language learning and translation emerges at the interface between Arabic-speaker Kamila and her fragile emotional condition:

> Kamila types in the word 'Happy' on her online translator even though it is a familiar word that she learned at school. It sounds like the narrator is using the soft Arabic "Ha", but Kamila can only manage the harsher Arabic "Haa". She decides that 'happy' requires too much effort. She reaches for her English dictionary, lets the pages fan through her fingers so that the air from it fans her face, then she stops, rotates her finger above the page and stabs it on a word. 'Avitaminosis'. Kamila thinks the word sounds like a Pharaoh's name. Her finger leads her into the definition: "Condition resulting from deficiency of one or more vitamins." The dictionary drops from her hands and she closes her eyes.

The digital translator enunciating the 'Ha' of 'Happy' 'requires too much effort' - it is out of reach for her native Arabic tongue. The English paper dictionary, in turn, provides relief in its haptic qualities as a material object that can be fanned and stabbed and generate new language seemingly at random. The choice of this medical term in the skein of the whole story, which weaves mental health into discussion of grief and language learning, is not random, however. Its aesthetic briefly evokes the grandeur of ancient Egypt. Its medical definition then foreshadows the physiological examinations and profound emotional loss Kamila experiences in the following paragraph. The effort of learning a language, translating, and editing using digital and paper tools is not separate from the embodiment of affect. This idea, generated expressively through this reading of Morris' story, gains further power when approached through the history of Cameroonian multilingualism discussed in what follows. I am suggesting here that a purely sociological or materialist historical account of contemporary African literary initiatives is incomplete when it comes to documenting their shapeshifting, multilingual interventions in world literary space.

Literary Translation Workshops in Multilingual Cameroon: Background, Antecedents, and Parallels to the Bakwa Workshop

The political and cultural relationship between anglophone and francophone Cameroonians has led to violent conflict in the Northwest and Southwest regions of the country and the self-declaration of an independent state of Ambazonia in 2017. Emerging from this historical context are 'contested identities that are by necessity in flux' and 'cannot be contained or confined within state-sanctioned acts of linguistic terrorism and sociopolitical repression'.[167] The 'anglophone problem' in Cameroon, as it is often referred to, is a legacy of German, British, and French control of the region. Following the defeat of Germany in World War I, Britain and France were given mandates over Germany's African colony of Kamerun in the Treaty of Versailles. This resulted in the varying imposition of colonial languages and education systems. Since independence, there have been active movements working towards independence, federalism, and unification in the country's ten regions. French is the principal lingua franca in eight of these regions; English is spoken by less than 20 per cent of the

---

[167] Nfah-Abbenyi, 'Am I Anglophone?', p. 182.

population, while in urban centres such as Yaoundé, anglophones and francophones live alongside each other. President Paul Biya has been in power since 1982 and is frequently accused of neglecting the demands of the minority anglophone population. Raphaël Thierry notes the 'impermeability' that has persisted between the anglophone and francophone book markets in Cameroon into the early twenty-first century.[168] Alongside the official languages of English and French, more than 250 African languages are spoken (including 55 Afro-Asiatic languages, 169 Niger-Congo languages, 4 Ubangian languages, and 2 Nilo-Saharan languages). The most spoken are Ewondo and Fulfulde, along with Cameroonian Pidgin and varieties of Camfranglais which act as lingua franca in urban settings.[169]

Independent publishing infrastructure has historically found ways to navigate and accommodate African multilingualism both nationally and transnationally. In rich histories of periodical culture and anthologisation, translators have signalled lines of connection, anti-colonial solidarity, post-independence aspirations, politicised ideas of continental unity, and forms of Black Internationalist *décalage*.[170] These imperatives have operated relatively independently from the cogs of Northern publishing apparatus. Writing in the landmark journal he launched in 1963, *Abbia: Revue culturelle camerounaise*, Bernard Fonlon insisted on the need for individual bilingualism, as well as state bilingualism, in the process of Cameroonian political, economic, technical, social, and cultural development. He notes that Cameroon is 'the country where linguistic confusion has reached its paroxysm', yet 'the insistent demand for national languages to transport African thought should not be simply dismissed as incoherent words of blinkered nationalism'.[171] Endogenous African languages, including those with relatively few speakers, 'authentically connect those who speak them to the African soil and past'.[172] Linguistic education, according to Fonlon, will lead in turn to autochthonous development. He makes no explicit

---

[168] Thierry, *Le marché*, pp. 239–42.

[169] For further linguistic context, see Ubanako and Anderson, *Crossing*. On publishing in African languages, see Thierry, *Le marché*, p. 277.

[170] Edwards, *Practice of Diaspora*.

[171] Fonlon, 'Pour un bilinguisme', pp. 18–21. My translation.   [172] Ibid., p. 22.

mention of translation in this article, though *Abbia* was bilingual and featured extensive translated literary and non-literary material.

The only evidence of translation training provision in the pages of *Abbia* is a report on an 'inter-African' translation workshop which took place in Libamba in 1963 and focussed on Bible translation. It was attended by sixty-six participants, including thirty-seven Africans, and forty-seven African languages were represented. Tutors included representatives from the American Bible Society, Wycliffe Bible Translators, Summer Institute of Linguistics, and the Federal University of Cameroon. The influential translation theorist Eugene Nida – best known for his development of the concept of 'dynamic equivalence' – was among the teaching staff.[173] The influence of Bible translation on translation theory and practice in Cameroon and more broadly on the continent is significant not only because of its role in developing language orthographies and the academic discipline of linguistics globally but because of the sizeablè material resources it has continued to benefit from in the post-independence period and up to the present day. Contemporary literary production operates in counterpoint to this embedded culture of translation and language pedagogy, yet connecting the two is a reminder of the asymmetrical distribution of resource connected to alphabetical literacy.

Long institutional histories of multilingual alphabetic literacy underpin expressive, cosmopolitan horizons in literary production and reception and structural contexts of knowledge production and circulation. Scholarship on missionary publishing, including debates about agency, translation, language, and orthographies, has highlighted the epistemic legacies of Christianity across the continent.[174] In the transhistorical contexts of coloniality/modernity, theories of world literature and the literary itself require fuller awareness of this dimension of the material, lived dimensions of multilingualism. A project of interlingual literary translation between some of the 250 indigenous languages of Cameroon coexists with the enduring dominance of and significant foreign funding for Bible translation

---

[173] Anon, 'Le séminaire', p. 164.
[174] See, for example, Mudimbe, *Invention*, pp. 44–83; Thierry, *Le marché*, p. 225; Ashuntantang, 'Publishing and Dissemination', p. 252.

and associated linguistic work led by missionaries, especially in rural areas of the country, working for large-scale organisations such as SIL (Summer Institute of Linguistics) and CABTAL (Cameroon Association for Bible Translation & Literacy).[175] This point connects to longer running discussions concerning 'pragmatic' or 'everyday' literacy embedded in rural communities more widely across the African continent. Hierarchies of aesthetic value have continued to render such ways of reading, writing, and translating largely invisible in discussions of comparative and world literature, despite rigorous empirical studies by scholars of African print cultures and African linguistics. Though there is little overlap in their everyday work, these institutional contexts surrounding 'functional' literacy and translation continue to shape access to African languages as tools of translation in Cameroon (and elsewhere in the global South). A more multidirectional, nuanced awareness of the role of organised religion in the multilingual print cultures of Cameroon signals the lived contingency of the language question, beyond the politics of the global literary marketplace.

Feasibility Study, Focus Groups, and Workshop Overview
The location of literary translators often determines, and is determined by, access to resources of money and time to work and develop their practice. This argument was reaffirmed by Georgina Collins' scoping and feasibility study, commissioned in 2017 as part of a UK ESRC (Economic and Social Research Council) project on creative writing and literary translation training and mentorship opportunities.[176] Collins interviewed more than sixty translators, academics, writers, publishers, and students in Dakar,

---

[175] Like CABTAL, SIL's current main funder is the Wycliffe Foundation, an American organisation founded in 1942 and now headquartered in Singapore. According to their website, SIL is currently involved in more than 1,660 active language projects, representing 1.07 billion people in 162 countries.

[176] I initiated and led this project until April 2018 when Madhu Krishnan took on the leadership role during my maternity leave. I am grateful for the solidarity shown by colleagues and project partners in enabling the work to continue at that time and since.

Saint Louis, Abidjan, and Yaoundé and produced a bilingual report, translated into French by Edwige Dro, and freely available online.[177] This scoping work gauged conversations concerning literary translation training and mentorship in these three countries. One finding was that literary translation remained undervalued and largely invisible as a creative practice in Cameroon, despite high levels of in-country professional expertise and courses in translation in comparison to Senegal and Côte d'Ivoire. There are at least three MAs in Translation available at universities in Cameroon aimed at producing professional translators working for the bilingual state.[178] While many students write on literary translation for their dissertations, students interviewed as part of this research expressed the difficulty of breaking into literary translation, with most going on to work as translators of commercial, legal, and technical texts, or producing bilingual government documentation.[179] The research underpinning the report highlighted the scarcity, complexity, and fragility of funding mechanisms for literary translation as part of the local publishing infrastructure. Interviewees registered the contrasting multilingual landscapes across the three locations concerned and identified opportunities and necessary stakeholders for developing a programme of literary translation training, including the need to incorporate non-academic institutions and live literature events (such as spoken word performances, translation slams, oral performance of translations, and translation prizes).

The complex multilingual situation in Cameroon was amplified further during our series of focus group and planning meetings with individuals who had been involved in the feasibility study and their further networks, four months prior to the Bakwa translation workshop. These included academics from the Universities of Yaounde I, Bamenda, and Buea; students on the MA in Translation at Yaounde I; established professional translators; emerging translators; staff from the Bible translation

---

[177] Collins, *Feasibility Study*.
[178] There are MA degrees at Université de Yaoundé I; University of Buea-ASTI (Advanced School of Translators and Interpreters); and at the private ISTI (Institut Supérieur de Traduction et d'Interprétation) in Yaoundé.
[179] Collins, *Feasibility Study*, p. 24.

organisations SIL and CABTAL; and members of the National Commission for the Promotion of Bilingualism and Multiculturalism. Throughout these meetings, which largely focussed on translation between English and French and planning for the upcoming Bakwa workshop, the question of local languages was of course present. The urgency of the armed conflict along anglophone/francophone lines in Cameroon at times eclipses the broader context of African language politics. One focus group participant, the independent publisher Rita Bakop, remarked: 'We live in a context where two cultures, well two linguistic cultures, are constantly coming to blows. We must help them to live together.'[180] Apart from the Bible translation specialists, there was little consensus on the feasibility – or even desirability – of translating into and out of local languages, pidgin, or Camfranglais. Participants expressed concern around the lack of standardisation of these languages, many of which do not have standardised orthographies.[181] Some focus group participants commented that incorporating these languages into the workshop might invite accusations of 'tribalism' or ethnic favouritism. One focus group participant, Dr Ndé mu Fopinn, a linguistics specialist in Ngemba (around 500,000 speakers), has translated *Les fables de La Fontaine* into that language, as well as publishing dictionaries and a grammar of the language and translations from Bulu and Bamileke. He was planning to translate *Hamlet* and Corneille's *Le Cid* and remained adamant that literary translation into local languages is not only possible but a necessary act. Challenged by younger translators present on his choice to translate classics of the Western European canon, this

---

[180]   My translation.

[181]   Again, the perspective among Bible translation organisations active throughout the country is very different. To date, CABTAL's translators have produced the New Testament in twenty-four languages, with forty-two language orthographies developed overall in Cameroon. There are significant historical differences here. In British-ruled regions of Cameroon, some primary education took place using endogenous languages (Douala and Mungaka/Bali, as well as Pidgin). Textbooks were prepared in these languages. German Protestant missionaries also organised vernacular schools widely (Duala, Bulu, Bassa, Wondo, Bangangte, Bamum) (Mbassi Manga, 'Cameroon', p. 137).

conversation highlighted the particular translation expertise of applied linguists, with their knowledge of African language orthographies. It also anticipated discussions that would re-emerge at the workshop itself regarding canonicity and (re)translation.

The Bakwa literary translation workshop itself took place over five days in October 2019 at the Campost post-office building in the Biyem-Assi district of Yaoundé and was followed by a one-day conference on literary translation at the Muna Foundation. The workshop was convened as part of a collaborative 'Creative Writing and Translation for Peace' project with the University of Bristol, funded by a UK Arts and Humanities Research Council grant led by Madhu Krishnan as principal investigator. As co-investigator, I focussed on the translation strand, building from the feasibility study and focus groups.[182] The project aimed to mentor writers and translators, with the aim of improving cultural dialogue between anglophone and francophone Cameroonians in the context of ongoing civil conflict. Planned with the Bakwa director Dzekashu MacViban and established literary translators Edwige Dro, Georgina Collins, and Ros Schwartz, the workshop followed a creative writing workshop convened by Billy Kahora and Edwige Dro in June of the same. Both Bakwa workshops were followed by a three-month period of online mentorship leading to the publication of a bilingual (French–English) anthology of new writing, *Your Feet Will Lead You Where Your Heart Is/Le crépuscule des âmes sœurs*, grouping the ten stories produced by the creative writing workshop participants, and their translations.[183]

There were thirteen translation workshop participants, six working into French and seven into English. Participants were selected from a pool of

---

[182] For further reflection on the politics of these funding mechanisms, and in particular the related narrative concerning research 'impact' in the UK, see Bush, Krishnan, and Wallis, 'Print Activism'.

[183] MacViban and Njinyoh, *Le crepuscule*. The creative writing mentors were Edwige Dro, Billy Kahora, Babila Mutia, Florian Ngimbis, Yewande Omotoso, and Marcus Boni Teiga. The translation mentors were Georgina Collins, Edwige Dro, Sika Fakambi, Roland Glasser, Mona de Pracontal, and Ros Schwartz.

more than fifty applications based on a letter of motivation and sample translation. The majority of applicants were practising professional translators who had studied translation at undergraduate, MA, or (in one case) PhD level. Over five intensive days, they worked practical exercises on topics including translating poetry, translating non-standard language, translating orality, translation and creative writing, and translating children's literature. Each day included a lunchtime session with invited publishing professionals to discuss publishing and funding literary translations and ended with a plenary reading group session, drawing on one of the theoretical readings provided to supplement participants' existing knowledge of translation theories. Steps towards the anthology publication were gradually woven into the week's schedule.[184]

Pedagogy in Literary Translation Workshops

Creative writing workshops developed rapidly over the twentieth and early twenty-first centuries as privileged venues for developing and reflecting on the craft of writing.[185] Literary translation workshops, such as those run by the British Centre for Literary Translation (BCLT) or championed by the American Literary Translation Association, have also expanded their reach globally in recent decades. The BCLT workshop model, which brings writers into dialogue with authors, has been adapted in China, India, and Indonesia, driving closer dialogue between writers and literary translators and expanding the understanding of both processes.[186] Literary translation training opportunities have also become increasingly commodified as products which tend to reproduce North/South asymmetries in their availability and cost. Despite their evident benefits at an individual level and increasing availability of scholarships, many (including the 'Bristol Translates' summer school now based at my own institution, the University of Bristol) remain symptomatic of the contradictions of

---

[184] For the full schedule and example activities from the workshop, see Collins, *Resource Pack*.

[185] On the role of these workshops in shifting the centre of the anglophone literary canon on the African continent, see Kiguru, 'Literary Prizes', pp. 210–11.

[186] José, 'Translation Plus', pp. 11–13.

neoliberal university culture, residual imperial cartographies, and an international literary industry found elsewhere in the transnational circuits of British-founded literary festivals.[187] Workshops nonetheless retain an aura of the artisanal process. They offer 'hands-on' exercises and continuous dialogue with an experienced translator and fellow apprentices. They also offer moments of joy and surprise, as seen in numerous blogs testifying to the transformative, even emancipatory, pleasure of such experiences. There remains relatively little critical literature on literary translation workshops, or specific case studies of how these workshops operate and the kinds of creative and professional practice they might foster or inhibit.[188]

While informal writing mentoring has pre-existed in myriad forms, formalised creative writing workshops emerged in university education in the early twentieth century. Creative writing workshops on the African continent have flourished in the 2000s, often benefitting from foreign funding and leading to the publication of an anthology while galvanising new networks and forms of creative expression.[189] These workshops act as platforms and as living, temporally bound synapses in the networks that underpin the contemporary African literary scene. They create rare time and space for writing and developing small-scale and embodied forms of critique, where gesture, breath, and non-verbal communication contribute to shared readings. Literary translation workshops offer similarly rare, and therefore valuable, time and space for acts of critical generosity and engaged pedagogies of hope. A pedagogy of hope, understood in a Freirean sense, entails 'opening up to the thinking of others' and understanding knowledge production and interpretation as an immanently collective process.[190]

Such workshops do not clearly map onto the institutionalisation of Translation Studies as an academic discipline. During the focus group

---

[187] Literary translation centres and workshops in Holland (Amsterdam), Spain (Tarazona), France (Arles), and Germany (Straelen) have been unattached to universities, while translation workshops at Iowa predate the emergence of the BCLT.

[188] Washbourne, 'Teaching'; Venuti, *Translation*.

[189] Kiguru, 'Literary Prizes'; Bwa Mwesigire and Krishnan, 'Creative Writing'.

[190] Freire, *Pedagogy of Hope*, p. 110.

meetings, several students and young translators described their formal training via MA courses in Cameroon, and the dominance of European theories over African theories of translation. They commented on the translation of the national anthem and echoed Bernard Fonlon's ideas on translation as a driver of national unity and development. In a sceptical account of literary translation workshops, Lawrence Venuti notes that 'the typical translation workshop is staffed by a poet-translator or a professional translator who inexorably and often unwittingly imposes his or her own aesthetics on student translators'.[191] This description follows the defence of foreignising translating strategies as an ethical imperative. Workshops characterise what Venuti describes as 'belletristic' approaches invested in abstract, under-theorised notions of aesthetic value. In a foreignising approach, aesthetic value is deeply contingent and cannot be assumed or universalised. However, such an argument concerning literary translation workshops marginalises the critical and theoretical capacity of writers (and writing), translators (and translations), and workshop participants. It presupposes what Paulo Freire memorably theorised as a banking model of pedagogy, with students as empty receptacles for knowledge. It maintains furthermore that critical theoretical work falls within a specific realm of discourse (abstract, scholarly, verbal, written) and takes place in the academy. In what follows, I make a divergent argument concerning the kinds of theoretical labour that literary translators undertake and which became visible in the Bakwa workshop space.

This argument connects to prominent strands in decolonial thought that collapse the distinction between theory and practice, as well as recent discussions of African poetry that have affirmed the theoretical capacity of literature itself. Suhr-Sytsma asserts that, across forms of lyric animism, left pan-Africanism, and diasporic poetics (each accented by metaphysics, politics, and intersectionality), to theorise 'is not to abstract so much as to think in memorable form'.[192] As we have already seen in the case of David Diop's transatlantic trajectories – translated poetry becomes a means of thinking racialised experience 'in memorable form', emphasising the importance of embodied presence, as well as intellectual subjectivity in the task of

---

[191] Venuti, *Translation*, p. 243.   [192] Suhr-Sytsma, 'Theories', p. 602.

theorising violence. The situated case study of a literary translation work-shop taking place in Yaoundé in 2019 provides a helpful example for understanding tutors' and participants' thinking about, and *in*, literary form in order to theorise transcultural and multilingual existence in Cameroon and beyond.

Multilingual Pedagogy at the Bakwa Literary Translation Workshop

Translators' craft and critical processes of reflection are entwined with institutional contexts of cultural production *and* their subjective embodied experience.[193] In the case of the Bakwa workshop, both students and tutors were led to reflect on the politics of source and receiving language/culture. Banal value judgements of what was 'good' or 'bad' writing rarely surfaced without further qualification. The initial focus was on the 'boldness' of the translator's voice, and what this meant in practice and against the context of local and global publishing ecologies and language politics. Workshop participants were encouraged to think critically and independently about their work, rather than being delivered a 'product' or 'method' (in a banking model of education). Moreover, rather than the tutors' authority becoming 'repressive and counterproductive', the tutors were themselves challenged in profound and transformative ways.[194]

On the opening day, the English–French tutor Edwige Dro provided students with extracts from Trần Thị NgH's short story 'The Sitting Woman' (translated from Vietnamese to English by Kaitlin Rees), Adaobi Tricia Nwaubani's *I Do Not Come to You by Chance*, Jane Austen's *Emma*, and John Reed's translation of Ferdinand Oyono's *Une vie de boy*. The fast-flowing discussion encouraged students to think about literary voice foremost, including in translated texts. The opening reading of 'The Sitting Woman' immediately led to a discussion of cultural compe-tence in relation to the following extract:

---

[193] To give a very concrete example, one participant in the Bakwa workshop had a disability (undisclosed until the final day) which affected their ability to engage in class discussions.

[194] Venuti, *Translation*, p. 243.

> At fourteen I fell in love with a man, a writer, older than me
> by thirteen years, already with a family. He resembled
> a young Anthony Perkins, that guitar-playing wanderer
> who roams the forest and happens upon the doe eyes of
> Audrey Hepburn in the foliage. At twenty-one I lost my
> virgin body to a person who specialized in the old *lục
> bát* verse, older than me by fifteen years, also like
> Anthony Perkins, also with a wife.[195]

The tutor asked: did students feel able to translate this text? How would
they find out what was meant by 'old *lục bát* verse'? How would they
convey the allusion to the narrator's older lovers, who resemble 'a young
Anthony Perkins'? How far could they identify with emotions of the
narrator, as she described her experience of falling in love with a series of
older men? One student commented on the importance of memory in this
passage and a melancholic tone towards the end. Another described the
filmic elements of the scene and informed fellow participants (who were not
all aware) that Audrey Hepburn was an American actress and so it could be
inferred that Anthony Perkins was too.

In contrast, most students expressed stronger emotional identification
and greater confidence with the second extract provided, from a bestselling
novel by the Nigerian writer Adaobi Tricia Nwaubani. Nwaubani's novel is
the story of Kingsley, an unemployed university graduate who is disillu-
sioned on graduation to find that the only pathway to economic success is
through email scams and the improvised money-making antics of his Uncle
Boniface. One workshop participant felt she could 'situate herself' in the
text as it referred to 'our culture': 'this text transmits what we often
experience in our families.' They could recognise some of the linguistic
expressions in Nigerian Pidgin. Some felt they understood the second text
better, and therefore could translate it more competently. This discussion
created space for the tutor to intervene critically, pushing back against
homogenised ideas of African culture. Her theoretical intervention

---

[195] NgH, 'Sitting Woman', n.p.

encouraged deeper self-reflection, warning against simplistic identification or false illusions of cultural competency and translatability.

There followed some discussion of the central theme of money and material wealth in this extract from the novel. Uncle Boniface's wealth animates his pretention and scorn for the university-educated Kingsley. How, the participants asked, could they grasp these two voices in the dialogue? One picked up on the invocation provided in the workshop's opening session: to be 'bold enough to defend our choices', encouraging others in the group to be persuasive, while respecting what the author may have intended. The dialogue between Boniface and Kingsley highlights economic relations through the formality of address, relationships of seniority, and implied social hierarchies. One participant noted:

> Our contemporary relationship to money appears in this text. Back in the day there was the class problem, as in aristocracy and proletariat. I feel like we don't have such a class conflict here [. . .] Today it's more about personal divisions, between individuals, we don't consider ourselves as a class. We consider ourselves as having succeeded, and the other person as a failure [. . .] Uncle Boniface is comparing himself to the father of this young man, and so he doesn't see himself as part of the aristocracy or bourgeoisie; he sees his own self-realisation [. . .] which the other guy's son demands. And he judges that it's not worth the cost. Today that's the rule, it's money; either you have money, or you keep quiet.[196]

Unpacking the language of class relations, the participant gestured to an atomisation of contemporary West African society on the basis of economic wealth and individualistic perceptions of success. Financial capital wields forms of social power. Though light-hearted in tone, the comment spoke to a broader misunderstanding underpinning some participants' participation in the workshop, which tutors were quick to correct – namely, that this

[196] My translation.

workshop, funded by a British grant body through a British university, could lead to lucrative work opportunities. Literary work as ethical endeavour, vocation, or leisure pursuit – like the idealistic intellectual ambitions of Nwaubani's protagonist, Kingsley – is only possible where basic material conditions (sufficient household income, support with duties of reproductive labour) allow it to exist as such. The tutor here pivoted to encourage the workshop participants to think of themselves as writers with creative agency, using this scene to think about the deeper levels of characterisation and narrative in play. They spoke of the naivety of this student character, Kingsley, faced with 'Cash Daddy', his uncle Boniface. When it came to their own translations and sharing these with the group, discussion of musicality, tonality, and register arose. How would they translate Uncle Boniface's dismissive expression that students such as his nephew have been sent to 'finish your brains on books'? How to handle the ambiguity of 'finish'? This phrase's puncturing of the symbolic prestige of completing undergraduate study, alongside its entrenched anti-intellectual sentiment, was difficult to render in French. Nonetheless, this opening exercise saw participants theorise class relations, sexuality and desire, Nigerian identities, wealth, fraud, and education in an era of neoliberalism through their individual translating practice and collective discussions.

In the second part of this session, participants were encouraged to reflect on an extract taken from the opening of John Reed's translation of Oyono's *Une vie de boy*. One commented that it was 'well translated', that Reed had 'a better command of English than us'. Another responded that Reed had made this 'more digestible' than the French source text, increasing the humour but also, as a third commented, losing something of the register. The narrative voice here is that of a young house servant recollecting past events. Reed shuns contractions and adopts expressions including 'I can still remember . . .' and 'oddly enough', but, as one participant commented, 'a boy doesn't speak like that here'. When provided with the French source text, some participants were surprised to find Oyono's writing was more formal than they imagined. 'Oyono forgets to incarnate his character', remarked one. This conversation led to reflection on register and how it could be retranslated for a contemporary readership, perhaps using Pidgin English. The participants wanted to make this text enticing for new readers by making the house boy's voice less 'élevé'. An expression such as 'I shall try it out' was 'flat' and lacked 'emotion', the 'je-ne-sais-quoi', which they hoped for when encountering Oyono's classic text in English translation. A term which led to more extended discussion was the translation of 'mangeur d'homme' (literally, 'eater of man') in the source text. Reed's rendering as 'cannibal' was flagged as problematic. The tutor, Edwige Dro, commented that she felt 'uncomfortable' in reproducing such justificatory language for colonialism, raising the question, 'should the translation be political?'. Dro spoke of not wanting to 'vautrer ma culture' (knock down my culture) – of finding a way to express nuance. Participants deconstructed the colonial discursive field surrounding anthropophagy, commenting on different ethnic groups, their hierarchies, and the ways in which discourse on eating human flesh functions as a way of expressing fear and power. Parallels might be drawn with long-standing discussions of postcolonial language politics and translation as an act of cannibalism.[197] Such metaphors are, of course, not uniquely African in any sense, given their rich history in Christian theology, and, especially, in Brazil, where they 'ring not a note of furious aggression but rather one of irreverently amorous devouring' derived from 'a non-Eurocentric way of conceiving spiritual force as inseparable from matter', a 'tribute to the other's strength' which simultaneously resists the default primary value of an 'original' or 'source'.[198] In Yaoundé, the conversation led to the tutor encouraging students to critique both Reed and Oyono. They asked where the line could be drawn between translating and rewriting and noted Reed's obvious ease with using the term 'cannibal', in contrast to their desire to show the depth of African cultures, making the book 'relevant to the current African context'. The resulting workshop task was devised by the tutor and students: to translate Reed's translation back into French *and* Oyono's text into English again, in order to compare their approaches. This example of engaged pedagogy meant students were deeply attuned to the aesthetics of the work as well as their ethical responsibility as literary translators speaking from within contemporary lived realities in Cameroon, yet aware of the 'high stakes' of translating 'Africa' within a global literary imagination dominated by reductive portrayals of the continent and its inhabitants.

---

[197] Campos, 'Anthropophagous Reason'.   [198] Vieira, 'Liberating Calibans', p. 96.

The daily plenary sessions reunited the two groups of translators around selected themes and readings, themselves derived from the focus group meetings. These discussions touched on topics of retranslation and the nature and politics of literary form (lexis, syntax, grammar, as well as narrative voice, tone, register, style, and imagery). One session returned to the narrative voice of Oyono's *Une vie de boy*. Perhaps, proposed one tutor, Oyono wanted to suggest that this boy could be an intellectual, a 'boy PhD', rather than assuming a naïve outlook on the world. Could they produce bold translations that were more than reactions to first translations they deemed poor or misjudged? The tutors encouraged humility. Dro suggested that they could only aim for contingent translations without guaranteed posterity. Participants pondered a familiar translating quandary: whether to adopt an 'archaeological' approach concerned with excavating the original intended effect on the reader or to be more creative and take greater freedom. At this point, Ros Schwartz commented on the availability of online research tools and their effect on accuracy. Whereas John Reed may have struggled to picture 'bâtons de manioc', translating it literally as cassava sticks, the workshop participants regularly ate bobolo, a dish of pounded cassava shaped in cylinders. Three days later, the students brought their Oyono translations to the plenary session. They had reflected on the role of Oyono's narrator's diary-writing. One participant read her translation of Reed and another commented that this still felt too elevated in its register. Her translation of 'race' as 'notre communauté' was picked up by others in the group. They discussed 'bande', 'tribe', or 'clan', and whether these terms were too generic or too restrictive in scale. How were they, as translators, to conceptualise collective identity without reproducing markers of colonial discourse? Could they do so while producing a translation with which they were personally satisfied? How, in essence, was this task enabling them to decolonise the languages they had at their disposal as literary tools? One tutor queried whether simply 'hommes' could be used, rather than 'cannibales'. Here, it was suggested that it was Reed's ease with 'cannibals' rather than the literal 'man-eaters' that brought in a European perspective to give maximum dramatic impact. The session conclusions emphasised participants' realisation of the time, effort, and self-questioning involved in literary translation as a practice of freedom. There may be imperatives to translate in ways which neutralise colonial or gendered violence contained in the source text. Rather than reinscribe or neutralise past violence, these translators found themselves compelled to deploy their voices and interpretative agency in ways which offer redress and repair.[199]

The question of freedom and multilingualism continued to arise across the workshop activities. One group was asked to translate an extract from Jane Austen's *Emma* for a Cameroonian audience. After a period of independent working, the plenary discussion began with the question of which French to translate into and the intended readership. The tutor, Edwige Dro, outlined the risks of falsely universalising (and thereby neutralising) the target language when translating literary texts into French. Dro (an Ivorian national) spoke of translating into *français ivorien populaire*, rather than Nouchi. Several participants decided to translate into *français camerounais* (one mentioned an intended young, female readership), while another opted for Camfranglais. Multiple forms of French were immediately in play in a way which participants felt was not often the case in published translations they had encountered. Participants commented on the history of French in sub-Saharan Africa and the rigorous 'forme carrée' of French taught in schools and insisted on by parents ('un français châtié'). One of the resulting Austen translations was Ray Ndébi's Camfranglais version, performed to enthusiastic applause and laughter against the sound of an afternoon rainstorm.

Mon frère, Emma Woodhouse était mo, wise au school et très porteuse. Elle vivait dans la mort de la villa, man, c'est comme si nous on était seulement came l'accompagner. Massa, vingt-et-un ans déjà qu'elle life sans stress.	Emma Woodhouse, handsome, clever, and rich, with a comfortable home and happy disposition, seemed to unite some of the best blessings of existence; and had lived nearly twenty-one years in the world with very little to distress or vex her.

---

[199] For further discussion of translation as reparation, see Bandia, *Translation*.

(Cont.)

Elle et sa big étaient les seuls munas d'un pater genre trop peace. Depuis que sa réssé s'est married, c'est elle qui a begin à gérer et les ways du vieux, même comme elle était encore mbindi.	She was the youngest of the two daughters of a most affectionate, indulgent father; and had, in consequence of her sister's marriage, been mistress of his house from a very early period.
Jane Austen, *Emma*. [Translated into Camfranglais by Ray Ndébi, 2019].[200]	Jane Austen, *Emma*.

Ndébi's translation could provide ample spark for discussion of translation and adaptation, contact languages, and the theorisation of world literature as that which 'gains' in translation or retains inherent untranslatability. As Gillian Dow notes, several recent translations of Austen's novels have suffered from the 'flattening' effect of a global literary marketplace dominated by English that positions these texts (and their paratext) via their film adaptations in the late twentieth and early twenty-first centuries.[201] Ndébi's translation invites close rereading of Austen's deft prose, irony, and witty characterisation. The narrator's address ('man', 'massa') invites a friend to share the beginning of a juicy piece of gossip. Gendered as male, this gossip speaks of informal social spaces of confidence and pleasure. Where Said unpacks the covert symbolism of the plantation economy in Austen's *Mansfield Park*, Ndébi's rewriting is a reparative and hopeful gesture of ownership, evincing its own bold aesthetic and humour, while forging new expressive pathways in Camfranglais. The translation invites readers to become aware of the contemporary literary scene and linguistic context from which this translation speaks. The workshop laughter

---

[200] Ndébi has since translated the entire first chapter of the novel into Camfranglais, making some extensive revisions. I have left here the version as it was presented at the workshop.

[201] Dow, 'Translations', p. 135.

emphasises the common experience of participating in transforming this text for a new readership. That transformation took place alongside shared conversations, meals, spaces, embodied temporality, and climatic conditions, which led to the multilingual live literary performance, differently experienced, and only partly captured on the digital recording. Sharing it here reaches back towards that archived experience and its transcendent, ephemeral joy.

Two-Way Learning in the Workshop Space: North/South Lessons

A contrasting example of the affective and theoretical learning was the discussion of workshop tutor Ros Schwartz's ongoing work on the translation of Max Lobé's *Loin de Douala* (2018), during which participants critiqued Schwartz's rendering of Cameroonian Pidgin.[202] Schwartz was commissioned to undertake the translation based on almost four decades of literary translation experience. Her backlist of more than 100 translated works of fiction includes titles by Ousmane Sembène, Fatou Diome, Tahar Ben Jelloun, Georges Simenon, and Antoine de Saint-Exupéry. Alongside others of her generation, Schwartz has played a significant role in promoting the visibility and professional rights of literary translators in the UK, through advocacy work with the Society of Authors, the Translators Association, and PEN Translates and her work in delivering literary translation training (notably a summer school which has run since 2011 in London, Warwick, and Bristol). This has resulted in more support for literary translators in preparing fair contracts, clarifying recommended rates of payment, and copyright guidance. We see a trace of this practical impulse to make translators visible in early June 1987, when Schwartz wrote to Heinemann to remind them, based on clause 10 of her contract for translating *Docker Noir*, that her name should appear on the jacket and title page, alongside that of Sembène.[203] The archives include correspondence with Clive Wake (who had taught Schwartz at the University of Kent), a very detailed reader's report on Schwartz's

---

[202] The translation, *A Long Way from Douala*, was published in spring 2021 by UK independent publishing house Hope Road Publishing.
[203] Letter from Ros Schwartz to Jane Harley, 1 June 1987, HEB 15/8, AWS/UR.

translation and reference to their meeting to discuss the work. Structural forms of privilege, as well as individual talent, cultural competence, and ability, shape literary translation as a craft, by determining access to resource and networks. Editorial advice (such as that between Wake and Schwartz) and the kinds of more formal mentorship that Schwartz has since offered and continues to offer to new generations of translators are an important reminder of the collective, time-intensive, and iterative dimensions of the labour surrounding literary translation for publication.

In the Bakwa workshop, participants offered their own mentorship to Schwartz. They commented extensively on her rendering of Lobé's Pidgin, as well as the translation of culturally specific terms for food. 'Sauce d'arachide' had become 'peanut sauce' in Schwartz's draft, rather than 'groundnut soup'. This was reminiscent of earlier criticisms of Reed's 'cassava sticks'. It provoked laughter in the workshop setting and the next day prompted a delivery of some of the soup itself. The session raised a lingering question concerning ownership of translations and the extractive dynamics of research undertaken for translation of African literary texts (or, indeed, any form of research, including the present book you are reading). Schwartz asked one participant to read the dialogue aloud, stressing the importance of cadence and musicality in Lobe's writing and how she was working on evoking this in the English. This was a moment in the workshop when learning was most overtly two-way: the tutor learning about specificity of Cameroonian French and English, while participants contemplated first-hand the kind of cultural *décalage*, as well as extended fine-grained efforts of drafting and redrafting, that shapes published translations. Schwartz subsequently decided to travel to Geneva to meet with Max Lobé and work in detail on the translation together, further signalling the kinds of resource and professional commitment that can characterise the work of well-established literary translators.

Interspersed between the workshop and plenary sessions were lunchtime sessions with local publishers and a translation slam. The latter is a live event which pits two translators against each other, each having translated the same extract from a prescribed novel in advance of the event. The audience is provided with the two translations and the source text, and the event involves each translator describing their decisions and defending their approach. Inspired by the model of poetry slams, such an event could encourage unhelpful competition by encouraging the audience to measure up the relative value of each translation. In the case of the Bakwa workshop, it proved a useful exercise in highlighting the translator's subjectivity and decision-making process. Two of the workshop facilitators (Ros Schwartz and Edwige Dro) prepared an English translation of an extract from Sony Labou Tansi's novel, *L'anté-peuple* (1983), in which we are introduced to the protagonist, Dadou, the headteacher of a girls' school. The first observation was the overall similarity of both translations. Both leaned towards a scatological register for the repeated 'moche' of the source text that gestures to Tansi's theme of rotten corruption; they played on sibilance ('marche du moche'), using 'shitty' or 'pissed off'. The final line of the translation saw Dro incorporate an intertextual allusion to Amos Tutuola's classic text *The Palm-Wine Drinkard* (1952).

Not that Dadou was afraid of destiny or that he wanted to save face. But all the same it was pathetic for a thirty-nine-year-old man to look as if he was following a girl – delightful as she most likely is – like a dog. [Translation by Ros Schwartz]	Not that Dadou feared destiny or wanted to save face, but it was a bit shitty to have the head of a 39-year-old man following a girl – delicious no doubt – the way dogs would. [Translation by Edwige Dro]	Non que Dadou eût peur du destin ou qu'il voulût sauver la face. Mais c'était tout de même moche d'avoir la tête d'un jeune homme de trente-neuf ans qui suit une fille – délicieuse sans doute – à la façon des chiens. [Sony Labou Tansi, *L'anté-peuple*, (Éditions du Seuil, 1983, pp. 13–14)].

In Dro's translation, Tansi's disembodied head echoes Tutuola's 'Complete Gentleman'. In Tutuola's text, this 'Complete Gentleman' is gradually reduced to a bodiless head, and finally a skull, as he returns his body parts to those who have lent them to him. He undertakes this transformation while tricking a woman who has followed him from the market to the forest. She will later be rescued by the narrator. Tansi's and Dro's reference inverts the gendered dynamic of that classic text, introducing intertextual humour and a surreal image to highlight the narrator's covert desire. In the slam discussion of translating agency, Dro set out her feminist approach at this point, reminiscent of the 'woman-handling' found in early work by feminist translators.[204] Schwartz's translation, with syntactical concision ('like a dog'), signals the pathos of this schoolteacher's ogling (and his sense of shame) in a crisp, polished interpretation of Tansi's prose, while bypassing this intertextual resonance.

The Bakwa workshop affirmed that the practice of the literary translator is fundamental in a context defined by protracted conflict. It reinforced the conviction held by Cameroonian writers and readers that literature continues to matter. It raised questions regarding the desirable linguistic scale of frame of reference for the literary translator of African literature and the extent to which that frame of reference is overdetermined by institutional contexts of the global literary marketplace. These questions continue to shape contemporary African translation imperatives. While the ruins, remnants, and traces of the colonial matrix of power (including its Cold War dimensions) shape the publication of literary translations, the onus is now on initiatives which work and move ahead with networked and informed optimism despite historical conditions and in the face of structural asymmetries. These initiatives use funding models which impinge on aspiration towards complete autonomy and remain overtly engaged in what has been termed (at times in reductive economic terms) a literary hustle.[205] As the follow-up mentorship period to the workshop demonstrated most clearly, it is the resource of time which remains elusive for literary translators working in Cameroon. Recommended rates of pay for literary translation are hard to come by. There is limited visibility for literary translation as

---

[204] Godard, 'Theorizing'.   [205] Brouillette, 'On the African Literary Hustle'.

a specific art form. Literary translation training and experience require long-term investment by international funding bodies in collaboration with national bodies and education institutions, as well as a commitment by publishing houses (themselves often small organisations running under considerable financial pressure) to nurture new translating talent. These large structures can support, without dominating or setting the agenda, independent local structures such as the recently created Association des traducteurs littéraires du Cameroun (LITAC).

Retranslation and Extroversion

The term 'extroversion' figures prominently in African literary studies – and in decolonial thought more broadly. It is theoretical shorthand for the ways in which literary texts and knowledge production more broadly in the global South connect to value systems generated in/from the global North. Texts do this in their form and aesthetics and in their mode of production and reception.[206] Thematic and formal features of these novels include liminality, intertextuality, and the figuring of language politics through translation. There is a temptation to place the concept of extroversion as one side of a familiar binary: extroverted, global, cosmopolitan, elite forms of knowledge versus the introverted, local/national, endogenous, popular forms of knowledge. However, as Eileen Julien argues, building on the work of Karin Barber, Stephanie Newell, and others, the extroverted novels which dominate the university syllabus and Northern perceptions of African literary production should be situated within a much denser understanding of the African literary ecology.[207] This ecology includes performance, popular genres, oral texts, ephemeral texts, and the digital literary realm, encompassing small magazines, Facebook Fiction, new media narratives, blogs, and social media platforms. Julien's account of the aesthetics of extroversion places particular emphasis on the importance of reception, without explicit reference to literary translation as a form of reading. As shown in Chapter 3, the translation of African literary 'classics' has historically

---

[206] Julien, 'The Extroverted'; Adesokan, *Postcolonial*.
[207] Julien, 'The Extroverted', p. 689.

been extroverted within the global literary marketplace. Examples from the Bakwa workshop register the location and theoretical agency of Cameroonian translators as readers. They show how translation – and the desire for retranslation – remains deeply connected to contemporary concerns in the Cameroonian linguistic and political landscape, while revealing the value of counter-hegemonic initiatives in the publishing space.

Several of the workshop participants remarked on an ongoing pattern which sees African novels published in the global North and then translated by translators based there. What also emerged rapidly during the workshop discussions – particularly around Ferdinand Oyono's novels – was a sense of dissatisfaction felt towards translations of African literary 'classics', perceived to be inaccurate and at times racist, dated, or jarring with readers' expectations and desires. This criticism spilled into contemporary translated literature. One participant mentioned the 'flat' French translation – especially of its Pidgin English – of Imbolo Mbue's global bestseller, *Behold the Dreamers*; another commented on the cultural blind spots of the American translation of Patrice Nganang's *Temps de chien*. While signalling the critical agency of their acts of reading, such frustrations expressed deeper-seated inequalities of access to the resources needed for literary labour (time, money, training, and mentorship opportunities). These conversations foregrounded the political dimensions and challenges of literary translation in the Cameroonian context. These challenges are not only a matter of cultural competence or transcultural literacy (of the sort vastly improved by access to online research tools, where funds for data are available and connectivity is consistent). They concern an ethics of literary identification and ownership of the means of literary production operating locally and transnationally. One way forward concerns long-term access to resources to develop the craft of literary translation. There has been relatively little professionalisation of literary translation (even, as is usually the case, as a secondary job) on the continent, as a further dimension of publishing infrastructure. This is at odds with the huge expansion of professional literary translation networks, institutional bodies, and workshops in the global North in the past two decades.

Whether undertaken for publication or not, retranslation is an important factor in the consecration of literary classics.[208] Published retranslations are, to a large extent, contingent on perceived market demand. To date, there have been twenty-one English retranslations of Flaubert's *Madame Bovary*. In 2020, Oxford University Press began to commission a third new English translation of Proust's *À la recherche du temps perdu*, less than a decade after Penguin Random House published the final volume of its much-feted new translation. Venuti comments (in relation to multiple English retranslations of Rilke), on the production of 'entropic interpretations' that reflect the dominant literary values of the translating culture, and decisions couched primarily in abstract terms of literary genius.[209] To date, there have been no published English-language retranslations of francophone African classic novels. *Things Fall Apart* remains the only African novel to have been published in two French translations, first in 1966 as *Le monde s'effondre* (by Michel Ligny for Présence Africaine), and then in 2013 as *Tout s'effondre* (by Pierre Girard for Actes Sud). Poland, Germany, and Spain all published retranslations long before 2013.[210] The decision to confide this urtext of African literature to Pierre Girard rested on Girard's experience and familiarity with the 'house style' of the French publishing house Actes Sud.[211] Given the obstacles to distributing the Actes Sud edition on the African continent, this highlights the default tendency for a French publisher to contract a French translator rather than seek conscious engagement with the kinds of French that this book might engage in translation on the African continent. Several participants in the Bakwa workshop and preparatory focus groups noted they had worked on extracts from *Things Fall Apart* while studying translation at university in Cameroon. While African

---

[208] On the uneven patterns of translation as consecration of francophone African 'classics', see Ducournau, *La fabrique*, pp. 324–8. On the case of literary translation into Swahili, also using Bourdieusian tools, see Talento, 'Consecration'. On the uneven consecration through translation of award-winning writing in Kiswahili, see Kiguru, 'Language and Prizes', pp. 406–10.
[209] Venuti, *Contra*, p. 63.   [210] Madueke and Rao, '*Le monde*', p. 532.
[211] Ibid., p. 535.

poetry has lent itself to frequent, often simultaneous, retranslations, African novels resist such initiatives due to structures of copyright.

The question of optimum 'time lag' in the retranslation of francophone African fiction is moot. As Edwige Dro stated during the Bakwa workshop, 'Tomorrow will need its own translation. Do what you need to do today.' Steemers suggests that retranslation is desirable every fifty years for 'major works'.[212] This suggestion is arbitrary, since, in reality, retranslation is rare and largely determined by perceived market demand (perceived, that is, by anglophone global North publishing houses). In recent years, American university presses have played a key role in publishing new translations of previously untranslated books in line with the institutional growth of postcolonial studies as well as Black and Africana studies in North American universities. Series such as Global African Voices (Indiana University Press) and CARAF (University of Virginia Press) have produced numerous new translations, most often translated by America-based academics and African literature specialists. These include English translations of texts by Abdourahman Waberi, Sony Labou Tansi, and Alain Mabanckou, as well as previously untranslated texts by 'first-generation' writers such as Mongo Beti.[213] Based on responses among Africa-based readers, English retranslations of many of the first generation of francophone African classics are overdue. Publishers willing to take a commercial risk and support translation into the multiple Frenches spoken on the continent face not only the thorny, perennial issues of rights, funding, and distribution but the question of who will translate these books. How can new networks of translators be fostered, when publishers frequently maintain their preferred 'go-to' stable of translators?

This raises questions over how texts are selected for translation (or retranslation) and – most importantly – how these translations then circulate for readerships on the African continent. As seen during conversations at the workshop, the answers depend on material resources, as well as the influence of perceived value and aesthetic taste in the literary field. Do texts deemed formally experimental or stylistically complex lend themselves to multiple translations, as

[212] Steemers, 'Francophone African', p. 79.　[213] Ibid., p. 80.

witnessed in the case of *Madame Bovary* or the prose of Sony Labou Tansi? Historically, the presence of social or political themes, or potential 'anthropological' readings, has attracted publishers to African literary texts more readily than matters of form and style.[214] When it comes to translations, the form and style of the source text are also determined by the potential forms of the target language and multilingual modes of reading of the target readership. This adds a further layer of decision-making and reflection to the publishing process. Aesthetic complexity is not only a characteristic of an 'original' to be carried across in the translation. It obtains and finds meaning in the composite languages and transcultural encounters of translations themselves, especially among readers based on the African continent, as seen in the example of Ndébi's translation of Austen. Given the many African forms of French and English, this means that the formal innovation and aesthetic value long associated with the recycling and reinvention of those languages (from Tutuola and Kourouma to Saro Wiwa and Tchak) are where innovative translations of the twenty-first century can find both momentum and new readership.

This closing discussion of retranslation leads specifically to the stated desire for new translations that express contemporary linguistic and cultural contingencies, rather than putative universality or abstract claims to modernity or aesthetic innovation. The project with Bakwa and subsequent follow-on activities, including the English translation of Hemley Boum's *Les jours viennent et passent* by Nchanji M. Njamnsi (to be published in September 2022 by Bakwa Books and Two Lines Press), signal how translators based in Cameroon are negotiating the kinds of extroversion and sociability enabled by the digital literary space, in turn revising local and transnational conversations about African literary translators' practice.

---

[214] Huggan, *The Postcolonial*; Ibironke, *Remapping*.

5 Conclusion

Debates concerning translators' identities have resurfaced recently through polemics concerning Amanda Gorman's Dutch and Catalan translators but have been covertly present in structural contexts of African literary production for much longer. These debates concern the capacity of translators to translate from beyond their implied cultural context and the forms of affective dissonance and frustration which this can provoke for both translators and readers. As I have outlined in the previous three chapters, translators' lives often tell a more complicated story. The material conditions for literary translators based on the African continent nonetheless remain an obstacle to fostering a more equitable and pluriversal ecology of knowledge. By determining who is able to translate literature for publication, these structural obstacles have political and aesthetic consequences.

This book has documented imperatives to translate African literature: from 'hackwork' for an earlier generation of expatriate translators and activist forms of anticolonial and anti-racist political praxis to (re)translation that centres Africa-based and digital readerships for contemporary literary activists in Cameroon. After parsing key issues in African literary translation, Chapter 3 reconsidered how literary meaning-making has historically operated via global Northern translation infrastructure (even where, as in the case of Wake, Reed, and Mpondo, this has been connected to variegated forms of anti-colonial and anti-racist politics). Chapter 4 offered a detailed account of the Bakwa literary translation workshop in order to extrapolate issues of resource distribution, pedagogy, and retranslation. The aims have been threefold: to give visibility to the optimism, creativity, and goodwill that underpin current literary translation initiatives on the African continent; to contribute to ongoing analysis of the uneven distribution of resources in world literary production, against a proposed horizon of the multilingual literary commons; and, lastly, to intervene in long-running theoretical and practical discussions traversing African, Comparative, and World Literary studies, as well as Translation Studies, concerning the aesthetics and politics of literary translation. Bringing together archival sources, close readings of literary texts, oral history, ethnographic, and participatory methods, my arguments will, I hope, stimulate further discussion and action concerning multilingualism, race, and material cultures of literary translation (in particular, issues pertaining to copyright, training, pedagogy, and retranslation).

Through their literary form and material circulation, African literary texts in translation enable readers to sense how African writers engage, express, and create a shared multilingual world. Readership is to be understood as highly contingent and unpredictable. My own readings, like those of Clive Wake, Edwige Dro, Simon Mpondo, Ray Ndébi, and Ros Schwartz, are not universal. Neither are these readings reducible to the individual positionality I sketched out in the book's Introduction and in the biographical overviews of these translators. At the very least, the readings offered over the course of this study seek to consistently engage with and acknowledge multiple readerships and readings as a means of registering the generative theoretical capacity of literature itself. In his discussion of extroversion, Paulin Hountondji describes 'endogenous' knowledge as that which is 'experienced by society as an integral part of its heritage, in contrast to exogenous knowledge which is perceived, at this stage at least, as an element of another value system'.[215] This definition depends, essentially, on subjective 'experience' and 'perception'. Transposed to the literary context, reception therefore remains paramount and, crucially, open to change. What is 'exogenous [. . .] at this stage at least' may already – or in the future – be perceived as 'endogenous' by differently sited audiences. This careful warning against static or polarised ideas of location and identity can be witnessed in American prisoners' responses to David Diop's poetry in English translation, in Mpondo's Seattle classroom, in Clive Wake's critical awareness – five decades on – of the limitations of some of his translations, and in Cameroonian translators' responses to Ndébi's Camfranglais translation of Jane Austen's *Emma*. It is a reminder that the textual interpolation of readers often occurs in surprising ways through form and multilingual aesthetics experienced in specific material contexts of production and reception. It speaks to Sousa Santos' description of translation as 'a living process to be carried out both with arguments and with the emotions deriving from sharing and differing under an axiology of care'.[216]

---

[215] Hountondji, *Endogenous*, p. 18. [216] Sousa Santos, *Epistemologies*, p. 213.

The etymological resonance between 'imperative' and 'imperial' may invite the discourse of command and control, both anathema to an ethics of care. I am not proposing a new set of imperatives for translators in this book but rather setting out the linguistic and translational imperatives already in existence – some more visible than others. The 'right' to read and speak about African literature is less significant here than addressing structural conditions which can appear intractable: reliance on funding from the global North, an enduring dominant focus on functional literacy and its developmentalist logic (by governments, NGOs, and Bible translation organisations), and the uneven conditions of literary labour. If translation, like decolonisation, is to remain more than a convenient metaphor (to return to Tuck and Yang's influential essay),[217] then these are issues that require further attention. Work on inequity and domination is deeply embedded in the practical politics of multilingualism, which academic scholarship ignores at its peril.

Literary translation continues to take place in formal and informal forms on the African continent, from university classrooms to missionary-led initiatives to online networks and the hype of contemporary literary collectives. I want to end by highlighting a further, contentious, avenue for future research: the relationship between digital technology and literary translation across multilingual African contexts. Might technology help address some of the material issues of resource raised in this book? The human-centred scale and ethics of artisanal translation in the workshop setting sits alongside the established role of digital tools in literary and translation futures.[218] A plenary discussion at the Bakwa workshop of post-editing neural machine translation tended towards scepticism. Participants minimised its potential role in literary translation, despite their familiarity with computer-aided translation (CAT). The use of CAT has been central to legal and professional translation industries for several decades and its potential use in literary translation has been a topic of recent interest,

---

[217] Tuck and Yang, 'Decolonization'.

[218] On the class and gendered dynamics of African digital literary spaces (focussing on Nigeria and Kenya), see Adenekan, *African Literature*.

particularly in translating genre fiction.[219] Market-leading software such as Trados functions by recognising word or phrase units in the source text and translating these consistently throughout a document. Neural translation, meanwhile, looks beyond units to the relationships between those linguistic units. It comes to its understanding of these relationships on the basis of a vast linguistic corpus (such as that of GoogleBooks), processing trillions of words and sentences to derive its artificial intelligence. The dominance of English and French texts published in the global North within these corpora is another important reminder of the asymmetries that persist in such ventures. What would a translation tool based entirely on African texts look like? Is a translation tool that permits and encourages overt forms of particularism (with all their definitional issues), and that disembodies the translating process, a utopian or dystopian prospect? It should at least be noted at this stage that Google Translate, Deep L, and Babel Fish offer often surprisingly readable translations of literary texts, though anathema to the artistic process of most human literary translators.[220] In most endogenous African-language translating contexts, moreover, the foundational issue of which corpora are used for CAT remains a major obstacle.

In the Bakwa workshop setting, digital translation technology opened up a conversation about what might encourage literary translators based on the continent in materially under-resourced contexts. Literary translation is a notoriously expensive process if paid according to rates recommended by international bodies. Could an initial CAT translation, followed by the editorial guidance of an Africa-based translator, be a possible way forward? The idea provokes strong reactions among many literary translators who emphasise the crucial creative act of producing the first draft. Technology may in principle offer fresh ways to negotiate multilingualism, but not while the institutional structures and fiscal impunity of big tech companies continue to reproduce inequities in the literary marketplace. In African literary

[219] Toral et al., 'Post-editing'.

[220] For a discussion of reactions to neural machine translation and human translation of Ahmadou Kourouma's *Allah n'est pas obligé* among participants in the 2016 Writivism Festival in Kampala, see Bush, Krishnan, and Wallis, 'Print Activism'.

contexts, technology's linguistic and literary implications invite further critical unpacking, including the risk of extending a potential further dimension of the 'Cold War paradigm' that Bhakti Shringarpure charts through the work of American big tech companies in the contemporary publishing landscape.[221] More immediately, then, further comparative discussion of literary translation training, mentorship, and collaborative team translation initiatives beyond Cameroon is needed, especially in African-language translation. What can be gleaned from the Bakwa workshop experience, given the particular language situation in Cameroon? What is working elsewhere on the continent and in the diaspora? With a vigilant eye to disparities in digital access across the continent, is the catalytic effect of the Covid pandemic opening up new opportunities for online mentorship and training, as well as critical collective translation? How are literary agents and publishing houses responding? How do translators based on the continent intervene in theoretical debates connected to multilingualism, translation, and decolonisation? Such questions suggest directions for reflection and future research which are far from exhausted, not least given the institutional growth of Translation Studies on the continent. This book has demonstrated how the agency of individual literary translators is entangled with multiple residual structures of power operating nationally and transnationally, including publishing infrastructure, state language policies, religious institutions, universities, and digital machine translation technology. Nonetheless, informed and digitally networked modes of optimism characterise current (re)translation imperatives on the African continent and signal numerous avenues for ongoing transdisciplinary and collective labour.

[221] Shringarpure, *Cold War*, p. 138.

References

Archival Sources

Clive Wake papers, University of Kent Special Collections, UK. (CW/K)

Clive Wake private papers. Includes typed proceedings of the 1958 'Writing and Society in Africa' seminar, held at University of Rhodesia and Nyasaland. (CW/P)

Dorothy Blair papers, University of Westminster Special Collections, UK.

Heinemann African Writers Series, University of Reading Library Special Collections, UK. (AWS/UR)

Higher Education in Africa collection, MSS. Afr. s. 1825 (120) (Box LXXVII, Memorandum of Clive Wake), Bodleian Library, Oxford, UK.

John Reed papers, Chetham's Library, Manchester, UK. (JR/C)

Interviews and Email Correspondence

James Currey, Interview (17 February 2011)

Susan R. Henderson, Email Correspondence, June 2021

Thomas Kinsella, Email Correspondence, August 2020

Clive Wake, Interview (25 June 2019) and Email Correspondence (June 2019 to July 2021)

Focus group participants, June 2019 (discussions convened by Georgina Collins, Madhu Krishnan and Ruth Bush): Prudence Lucha, Paule Ghislaine, Samuel Dongmo, Nde Fopin, Jean Takougang, Serge Auguste Massock, Sapa Bassong III Baruch, Sokeng Piewo Stephane Celeste, Valentine Ubanako, Charles Kouassen, Kisito Hona, Marcel Nyanchi, Rita Bakop, Arielle Kéwé, Nfor Edwin Njinyoh, Felicite Ette Enow, Tchouela Djatche Eder, David Awono, Kelese Emmaculate,

Nchanji M. Njamnsi, Wilfred Barry, Francis Mbara, Bolak Kari Mekwi, Keyeh Emmanuel Lufang, Frans Barah, Leah N. Mbua, Mbori Wilfred Fai; Ambassa Apollinaire, Chris Smoes, Sulee Tangko, Virginia Beavon-Ham

Organisers and participants of the Bakwa literary translation workshop, October 2019: Dzekashu MacViban, Edwige Dro, Ros Schwartz, Madhu Krishnan, Georgina Collins, Felicite Ette Enow, Hector Kamdem, Kidio Rolland Samni, Maison Bindzi Concorde Diane, Nchanji M. Njamnsi, Nfor Edwin Njinyoh, Zih James Kum, Fadimatou Nastainou Njapndounke, Jessie Judith Ndjeya Nkouetchou, Josépha Bamba, Marie-Hélène Ngoah Ngalle, Mariette Tchamda, Patient Xavier Nong, Ray Ndébi

Published Sources

Adenekan, S. *African Literature in the Digital Age* (New York: Boydell & Brewer, 2021).

Adesokan, A., *Postcolonial Artists and Global Aesthetics* (Bloomington: Indiana University Press, 2011).

American Literary Translation Association, 'Statement on Racial Equity in Literary Translation', www.literarytranslators.wordpress.com/2021/03/22/alta-statement-on-racial-equity-in-literary-translation/ (accessed 9 April 2021).

Anon, 'Le séminaire inter-africain de traduction de Libamba', *Abbia: revue culturelle camerounaise* 3 (September 1963), pp. 164–6.

Appiah, K. A., 'Thick Translation', *Callaloo*, 16:4 (1993), 808–19.

Apter, E., *Against World Literature: On the Politics of Untranslatability* (New York: Verso, 2013).

Apter, E., *The Translation Zone: A New Comparative Literature* (Princeton, NJ: Princeton University Press, 2006).

Ashuntantang, J., 'The Publishing and Dissemination of Creative Writing in Cameroon', in C. Davis and D. Johnson, eds., *The Book in Africa: Critical Debates* (Basingstoke: Palgrave Macmillan, 2015), pp. 245–66.

Awung, F. N., 'Representing African through Translation: Ferdinand Oyono's *Une vie de Boy* and *Le Vieux nègre et la médaille* in English', PhD thesis, University of the Free State, 2018.

Awung, F. N., 'Translating *Une vie de boy*: A Bourdieusian Study of Agency in Literary Translation', in J. Inggs and E. Wehrmeyer, eds., *African Perspectives on Literary Translation* (Abingdon, UK: Routledge, 2021), pp. 244–59.

Baker, M., 'Translation and Activism: Emerging Patterns of Narrative Community', *The Massachusetts Review*, 47:3 (2006), 462–84.

Bandia, P., 'On Translating Pidgins and Creoles in African Literature', *Traduction, Terminologie, Rédaction*, 7:2 (1994), 93–114.

Bandia, P., *Translation As Reparation: Writing and Translation in Postcolonial Africa* (Manchester: St Jerome Publishing, 2008).

Bassnett, S. and Trivedi, H., eds., *Post-colonial Translation: Theory and Practice* (Abingdon, UK: Routledge, 1999).

Batchelor, K., *Decolonizing Translation: Francophone African Novels in English Translation* (Manchester: St Jerome Press, 2009).

Batchelor, K., 'The Translation of *Les Damnés de la terre* into English: Exploring Irish Connections', in K. Batchelor and S.-A. Harding, eds., *Translating Frantz Fanon across Continents and Languages* (Abingdon, UK: Routledge, 2017), pp. 40–75.

Bejjit, N., 'The Publishing of African Literature: Chinua Achebe, Ngũgĩ wa Thiong'o and the Heinemann African Writers Series 1962–1988', PhD thesis, The Open University, 2009.

Benjamin, W., 'The Task of the Translator', in W. Benjamin, *Illuminations*, trans. Harry Zohn; ed. Hannah Arendt (New York: Harcourt Brace Jovanovich, 1968), pp. 69–82.

Blédou, L., Boum, H., Hane, K., and Thierry, R., 'A propos de traduction et de la circulation de nos œuvres', Roundtable at Aké Festival, 24 October 2020, www.youtube.com/watch?v=4Hz6hdTZUOA (accessed 26 October 2020).

Boum, H., 'La francophonie vue par l'écrivaine Hemley Boum: "Le Français nous appartient"', *L'Express*, 14 February 2018, www.lexpress .fr/culture/la-francophonie-vue-par-l-ecrivaine-hemley-boum-le-fran cais-nous-appartient_1984536.html (accessed 23 September 2020).

Brouillette, S., 'On the African Literary Hustle', *Blindfield Journal*, 14 August 2017, https://blindfieldjournal.com/2017/08/14/on-the-afri can-literary-hustle/ (accessed 10 January 2021).

Brouillette, S., 'On Some Recent Worrying over World Literature's Commodity Status', *Maple Tree Literary Supplement*, 18 (2017), www .mtls.ca/issue18/impressions/ (accessed 12 April 2021).

Brouillette, S., *Underdevelopment and African Literature: Emerging Forms of Reading* (Cambridge: Cambridge University Press, 2020).

Brouillette, S., *UNESCO and the Fate of the Literary* (Stanford, CA: Stanford University Press, 2019).

Bush, R., *Publishing Africa in French: Literary Institutions and Decolonization* (Liverpool: Liverpool University Press, 2016).

Bush, R., 'Publishing Francophone African Literature in Translation: Towards a Relational Account of Postcolonial Book History', in K. Batchelor and C. Bisdorff, eds., *Intimate Enemies: Translating Francophone Texts* (Liverpool: Liverpool University Press, 2013), pp. 49–68.

Bush, R., Krishnan, M., and Wallis, K., 'Print Activism and Translating African Literature: Conversations at Writivism 2016', *In Other Words: The Journal for Literary Translators*, 49 (2017), 46–55.

Bwa Mwesigire, B., 'What Is Literary Activism? (Or Who keeps the Housekeepers' House?)', *East African Literary and Cultural Studies*, 7:1–2 (2021), 10–22.

Bwa Mwesigire, B. and Krishnan, M., 'Creative Writing As Literary Activism: Decolonial Perspectives on the Writing Workshop', *Eastern African Literary and Cultural Studies*, 7:1–2 (2021), 97–115.

Cahill, C., Sultana, F., and Pain, R., 'Participatory Ethics: Politics, Practices, Institutions', *ACME*, 6:3 (2007), 304–18.

Campos, H., 'Anthropophagous Reason: Dialogue and Difference in Brazilian Culture', trans. O. Cisneros, in H. Campos, *Novas: Selected Writings*, ed. A. S. Bessa and O. Cisneros (Evanston, IL: Northwestern University Press, 2007), pp. 157–77.

Casanova, P., *The World Republic of Letters*, trans. M. B. DeBevoise (Cambridge, MA, and London: Harvard University Press, 2004).

Césaire, A., *Discourse on Colonialism*, trans. J. Pinkham (New York: Monthly Review Press, [1955] 2000).

Coetzee, C., *Accented Futures: Language Activism and the Ending of Apartheid* (Johannesburg: Wits University Press, 2013).

Coetzee, C., 'Unsettling the Air-Conditioned Room: Journal Work As Ethical Labour', *Journal of the African Literature Association*, 12:2 (2018), 101–15.

Coleman, A., 'Publishers Need More Black Translator Friends', *Words Without Borders*, January 2021, www.wordswithoutborders.org/article/january-2021-international-black-voices-publishers-need-more-aaron-robertso (accessed 23 January 2021).

Collins, G., *Feasibility Study: Literary Translation and Creative Writing Training in West Africa/Etude de faisabilité: Formation en traduction et creation littéraires en Afrique de l'Ouest*, trans. E. Dro. Report (2019), https://georginacollinsco.files.wordpress.com/2019/08/final-feasibility-study-english-1.pdf (accessed 14 April 2021).

Collins, G., *Literary Translation Training in West Africa: Resource Pack* (in press 2022).

Currey, J., *Africa Writes Back: The African Writers Series and the Launch of African Literature* (Oxford: James Currey, 2008).

D'Almeida, I. A., 'Literary Translation: The Experience of Translating Chinua Achebe's *Arrow of God* into French', *Meta: Translators' Journal*, 27:3 (1982), 286–94.

Damrosch, D., *What Is World Literature?* (Princeton, NJ: Princeton University Press, 2003).

Davis, C., *Creating Postcolonial Literature: African Writers and British Publishers* (Basingstoke: Palgrave Macmillan, 2013).

Davis, C. and Johnson, D., eds., *The Book in Africa: Critical Debates* (Basingstoke: Palgrave Macmillan, 2015).

Deltombe, T., Domergue, M., and Tatsitsa, J., *Kamerun!: Une guerre cachée aux origines de la Françafrique (1948–1971)* (Paris: La Découverte, 2019; first published 2010).

Diagne, S. B., *L'encre des savants: Refléxions sur la philosophie en Afrique* (Paris and Dakar: Présence Africaine and Codesria, 2013).

Diagne, S. B. and Amselle, J.-L., *In Search of Africa(s): Universalism and Decolonial Thought*, trans. A. Brown (Cambridge: Polity, 2020).

Diop, D., *Coups de pilon* (Paris: Présence Africaine, 1973; first published 1956).

Diop, D., *Hammer Blows and Other Writings*, trans. Simon Mpondo and Frank Jones (Bloomington: Indiana University Press, 1973).

Diop, D., *Hammer Blows*, trans. Simon Mpondo and Frank Jones (London: Heinemann Educational Books, 1975).

Djagalov, R., *From Internationalism to Postcolonialism: Literature and Cinema between the Second and the Third Worlds* (Montreal: McGill-Queen's University Press, 2020).

Dow, G., 'Translations', in J. Todd, ed., *The Cambridge Companion to Pride and Prejudice* (Cambridge: Cambridge University Press, 2013), pp. 122–36.

Ducournau, C., *La fabrique des classiques africains: Écrivains d'Afrique subsaharienne francophone* (Paris: CNRS Éditions, 2017).

Edwards, B. H., *The Practice of Diaspora: Literature, Translation and the Rise of Black Internationalism* (Cambridge, MA: Harvard University Press, 2003).

Fonlon, B., 'Pour un bilinguisme de bonne heure', *Abbia: Revue culturelle Camerounaise*, 7 (1964), 7–47, www.vestiges-journal.info/Abbia/ (accessed 23 January 2021).

Fouda, V.-S. , 'Ces martyrs dont personne ne parle au Cameroun', 31 May 2018, www.camer.be/68314/11:1/ces-martyrs-dont-personne-ne-parle-au-cameroun-par-le-prof-vincent-sosthane-fouda-cameroon.html (accessed 10 March 2021).

Fraiture, P.-P., 'Translating African Thought and Literature: Postcolonial Glottopolitics', in 'Translating African Thought and Literature', ed. P.-P. Fraiture, Special Issue, *Bulletin of the School of Oriental and African Studies*, 81:3 (2018), 405–12.

Freire, P. and Freire, A. M. A., *Pedagogy of Hope: Reliving Pedagogy of the Oppressed*, trans. R. Barr (London: Bloomsbury, 2014).

Galliand, É, ed., *Faut-il se ressembler pour traduire: Légitimité de la traduction, paroles de traductrices et traducteurs* (Paris: Double Ponctuation, 2021).

Gilmour, R. and Steinitz, T., eds., *Multilingual Currents in Literature, Translation, and Culture* (Abingdon, UK: Routledge, 2018).

Glover, K., '"Blackness" in French: On Translation, Haiti, and the Matter of Race', *L'Esprit Créateur*, 59:2 (2019), 25–41.

Go, J., *Postcolonial Thought and Social Theory* (Oxford: Oxford University Press, 2016).

Godard, B., 'Theorizing Feminist Theory/Translation', in S. Bassnett and A. Lefevere, eds., *Translation: History and Culture* (London: Frances Pinter, 1990), pp. 87–96.

Gould, R. and Tahmasebian, K., eds., *The Routledge Handbook of Translation and Activism* (Abingdon, UK: Routledge, 2020).

Halim, H., '*Lotus*, the Afro-Asian Nexus, and Global South Comparatism', *Comparative Studies of South Asia, Africa and the Middle East*, 32:3 (2012), 563–83.

Hardt, M. and Negri, A., *Commonwealth* (Cambridge, MA: Belknap Press, 2009).

Harris, A. and Hållén, N., 'African Street Literature: A Method for an Emergent Form Beyond World Literature', *Research in African Literatures*, 51:2 (2020), 1–26.

Harrison, N., 'World Literature: What Gets Lost in Translation?' *The Journal of Commonwealth Literature*, 49:3 (2014), 411–26.

Harrow, S., *Colourworks: Chromatic Innovation in Modern French Poetry and Art Writing* (New York: Bloomsbury USA, 2021).

Hountondji, P., ed., *Endogenous Knowledge: Research Trails* (Dakar: Codesria, 1997).

Huggan, G., *The Postcolonial Exotic: Marketing the Margins* (New York: Routledge, 2001).

Ibironke, O., *Remapping African Literature* (Basingstoke: Palgrave Macmillan, 2018).

Inggs, J. and Wehrmeyer, E., *African Perspectives on Literary Translation* (Abingdon, UK: Routledge, 2021).

Intrator, M. *Books across Borders: UNESCO and the Politics of Postwar Cultural Reconstruction, 1945–1951* (Basingstoke: Palgrave Macmillan, 2019).

Jaji, T., 'Our Readers Write: Mediating African Poetry's Audiences', *Research in African Literatures*, 51:1 (2020), 70–93.

José, N., 'Translation Plus: On Literary Translation and Creative Writing', *The AALITRA Review: A Journal of Literary Translation*, 10 (2015), 5–17.

Julien, E., *African Novels and the Question of Orality* (Bloomington: Indiana University Press, 1992).

Julien, E., 'The Extroverted African Novel', in F. Moretti, ed., *The Novel, Volume 1: History, Geography, and Culture* (Princeton, NJ: Princeton University Press, 2006), pp. 667–98.

Julien, E., 'The Extroverted African Novel, Revisited: African Novels at Home, in the World', *Journal of African Cultural Studies*, 30:3 (2018), 371–81.

Kane, Mohamadou, *Roman africain et tradition* (Dakar: Nouvelles Editions Africaines, 1982).

Keene, J., 'Translating Poetry, Translating Blackness', *Poetry Foundation*, www.poetryfoundation.org/harriet-books/2016/04/translating-poetry-translating-blackness#:~:text=In%20%E2%80%9CTranslating%20Poetry%2C%20Translating%20Blackness,based%20publishing%20organs%2C%20including%20literary (accessed 21 January 2021).

Kiguru, D., 'Language and Prizes: Exploring Literary and Cultural Boundaries', in M. Adejunmobi and C. Coetzee, eds., *The Routledge Companion to African Literature* (Abingdon, UK: Routledge, 2019), pp. 399–412.

Kiguru, D., 'Literary Prizes, Writers' Organisations and Canon Formation in Africa', *African Studies*, 75:2 (2016), 202–14.

Kinsella, T. and Tompkins, K., 'Stockton Stories: Simon Mpondo', www.stockton.edu/stories/simon-mpondo.html (accessed 20 July 2020).

Kotze, H. 'Translation Is the Canary in the Coalmine', 15 March 2021, https://medium.com/@h.kotze_94410/translation-is-the-canary-in-the-coalmine-c11c75a97660 (accessed 16 March 2021).

Krishnan, M., *Contingent Canons: African Literature and the Politics of Location* (Cambridge: Cambridge University Press, 2019).

Krishnan, M. and Wallis, K., 'Podcasting As Activism and/or Entrepreneurship: Cooperative Networks, Publics and African Literary Production', *Postcolonial Text*, 15:3–4 (2020), 1–26.

Lindfors, B., 'Book Review Forum: Remapping African Literature, by Olabode Ibironke', *Journal of the African Literature Association*, 14:2 (2020), 336–9.

Lizarríbar Buxó, Camille. '"Something Else Will Stand Beside It": The African Writers Series and the Development of African Literature', PhD thesis, Harvard University, 1998.

Mackenzie, C. G., 'The University of Rhodesia: A Re-appraisal', *Journal of Educational Administration and History*, 19:2 (1987), 62–71.

MacViban, D. and Njinyoh, N. E., eds., *Le crépuscule des âmes sœurs/Your Feet Will Lead You Where Your Heart Is* (Yaoundé: Bakwa Books, 2020).

Madueke, S. and Rao, S., '*Le monde s'effondre* ou *Tout s'effondre?* Traduire et retraduire Things Fall Apart en français', *Canadian Review of Comparative Literature/Revue Canadienne de Littérature Comparée*, 43:4 (2016), 531–50.

Marasligil, C., 'Uncaring. Reflections on the Politics of Literary Translation', Read My World blog, March 2021, www.readmyworld .nl/an-editors-note/ (accessed 9 April 2021).

Marzagora, S., 'African-Language Literatures and the "Transnational Turn' in Euro-American Humanities', *Journal of African Cultural Studies*, 27:1 (2015), 40–55.

Mbangue Nkomba, Y. P., 'Pétrole et jeu des acteurs dans la fabrication des politiques publiques des hydrocarbures au Cameroun', DEA, Université Yaoundé II, 2006, www.memoireonline.com/06/12/5980/m_Petrole-et-jeu-des-acteurs-dans-la-fabrication-des-politiques-publiques-des-hydrocarbures-au24.html (accessed 8 April 2021).

Mbassi Manga, F., 'Cameroon: A Marriage of Three Cultures', *Abbia: revue culturelle camerounaise*, 5 (1964), 131–44.

Mba Talla, M., 'Cameroun: Espace livres: Les mémoires post-mortem de Fochivé', *Mutations*, 18 December 2003, https://fr.allafrica.com/stor ies/200312180680.html (accessed 10 March 2021).

Mbembe, A., *On the Postcolony* (Oakland: University of California Press, 2001).

McCracken, J., 'In the Shadow of Mau Mau: Detainees and Detention Camps during Nyasaland's State of Emergency', *Journal of Southern African Studies*, 37:3 (2011), 535–50.

McDonald, P. D., *Artefacts of Writing: Ideas of the State and Communities of Letters from Matthew Arnold to Xu Bing* (Oxford: Oxford University Press, 2017).

McDonald, P. D., 'On Method: African Materials', *The Cambridge Quarterly*, 49:3 (2020), 303–12.

Miano, L., *L'impératif transgressif* (Paris: L'Arche, 2016).

Mignolo, W. and Walsh, C., *On Decoloniality* (Durham, NC: Duke University Press, 2018).

Mohdin, A., '"We Couldn't Be Silent": The New Generation behind Britain's Anti-racism Protests', *Guardian*, 29 July 2020, www.theguar dian.com/uk-news/2020/jul/29/new-generation-behind-britain-anti-racism-protests-young-black-activists-equality (accessed 9 April 2021).

Moore, G., 'African Writing Seen from Salisbury', *Présence Africaine*, 31:3 (1960), 87–94.

Mpondo, S., 'Assessing David Mandessi Diop', in *Hammer Blows and Other Writings*, trans. Simon Mpondo and Frank Jones (Bloomington: Indiana University Press, 1973). First published in *Présence Africaine* 75 (1970), 97–107.

Mpondo, S., 'From Independence to Freedom: A Study of the Political Thinking of Negro-African Writers in the 1960s', PhD thesis, University of Washington, 1971. Microfilm.

Mudimbe, V. Y., *The Invention of Africa: Gnosis, Philosophy and the Order of Knowledge* (London: James Currey, 1988).

Mukagasana, Y., *Not My Time to Die*, trans. by Z. Norridge (Kigali: Huza Press, 2019).

Munday, J., 'Using Primary Sources to Produce a Microhistory of Translation and Translators: Theoretical and Methodological Concerns', *The Translator*, 20:1 (2014), 64–80.

Nesbitt-Ahmed, Z., 'Reclaiming African Literature in the Digital Age: An Exploration of Online Literary Platforms', *Critical African Studies*, 9:3 (2017), 377–90.

Nfah-Abbenyi, J. M., 'Am I Anglophone? Identity Politics and Postcolonial Trauma in Cameroon at War', *Journal of the African Literature Association*, 14:2 (2020), 180–97.

Nfah-Abbenyi, J. M. and Doho, G., 'Fragmented Nation or the Anglophone-Francophone Problem in Cameroon', *Journal of the African Literature Association*, 14:2 (2020), 171–2.

NgH, T. T., 'The Sitting Woman', trans. Kaitlin Rees. *Words Without Borders*, November 2018, www.wordswithoutborders.org/article/november-2018-vietnam-the-sitting-woman-tran-thi-ngh-kaitlin-rees (accessed 24 January 2021).

Ngũgĩ, Mukoma wa and Murphy, L., eds. 'The African Literary Hustle', *New Orleans Review*, 43 (2017).

Ngũgĩ wa Thiong'o, *Decolonising the Mind: The Politics of Language in African Literature* (London: James Currey, 1986).

Niranjana, T., *Siting Translation: History, Post-Structuralism, and the Colonial Context* (Berkeley: University of California Press, 1992).

Norridge, Z. and Mukagasana, Y. *Not My Time to Die* (Kigali: Huza Press, 2019).

Nwaubani, A. T., *I Do Not Come to You by Chance* (London: Weidenfeld & Nicolson, 2009).

Ojo-Ade, F. *On Black Culture* (Ile-Ife: Obafemi Awolowo University Press, 1989).

Ostrom, E., *Governing the Commons: The Evolution of Institutions for Collective Action* (Cambridge: Cambridge University Press, 1990).

Parmar, I., *Foundations of the American Century: The Ford, Carnegie, and Rockefeller Foundations in the Rise of American Power* (New York: Columbia University Press, 2012).

Pene, F., 'Christian Mpondo: les misères d'un homme traqué', *Le Messager*, 3 March 2006, www.peuplesawa.com/fr/bnagendas.php?agid=39 (accessed 10 March 2021).

Phipps, A., P. Diamond, C. Doherty, S. Nock, and T. Sitholé, 'A Short Manifesto for Decolonising Language Education', in A. Phipps, *Decolonising Multilingualism: Struggles to Decreate* (Bristol: Multilingual Matters, 2019), pp. 5–16.

Popescu, M., *At Penpoint: African Literatures, Postcolonial Studies, and the Cold War* (Durham, NC: Duke University Press, 2020).

Quayson, A., *Calibrations: Reading for the Social* (Minneapolis: University of Minnesota Press, 2003).

Rabéarivelo, J-J. , *Translations from the Night: Selected Poems of Jean-Jacques Rabéarivelo*, ed. and trans. J. Reed and C. Wake (London: Heinemann Educational Books, 1975).

Ranger, T., *Writing Revolt: An Engagement with African Nationalism, 1957–67* (London and Harare: James Currey and Weaver Press, 2013).

Reed, J. and Wake, C., eds., *A Book of African Verse* (London: Heinemann Educational Books, 1964).

Reed, J. and Wake, C., eds., *An Anthology of African and Malagasy Poetry in French* (Oxford: Oxford University Press, 1965).

Reed, J. and Wake, C., eds., *French African Verse* (London: Heinemann Educational Books, 1972).

Reed, J. and Wake, C., eds., *A New Book of African Verse* (London: Heinemann Educational Books, 1984).

Reza, A., 'African Literary Journals in French and Portuguese, 1947–1968: Politics, Culture and Form', DPhil Thesis, University of Oxford, 2018.

106 *References*

Roeschenthaler, U. and Diawara, M., eds., *Copyright Africa: How Intellectual Property, Media and Markets Transform Immaterial Cultural Goods* (Canon Pyon: Sean Kingston Publishing, 2016).

Samoyault, T., *Traduction et violence* (Paris: Édition du Seuil, 2020).

Sapiro, G. 'Translation and Symbolic Capital in the Era of Globalization: French Literature in the United States', *Cultural Sociology*, 9:3 (2015), 320–46.

Sapiro, G. and Heilbron, J., 'Outline for a Sociology of Translation: Current Issues and Future Prospects', in M. Wolf and A. Fukari, eds., *Constructing a Sociology of Translation* (Amsterdam: John Benjamins, 2007), pp. 93–107.

Sarr, F., *Afrotopia* (Paris: Philippe Rey, 2016).

Sekyi-Otu, A., *Left Universalism, Africacentric Essays* (New York: Routledge, 2019).

Sembène, O., *Les bouts de bois de Dieu: Banty mam yall* (Paris: Pocket, 2013; first published 1960).

Sembène, O., *Gods Bits of Wood*, trans. F. Price (Oxford: Heinemann Educational Books, 1995).

Senghor, L. S., ed., *Anthologie de la nouvelle poèsie nègre et malgache de langue française* (Paris: PUF, 1948).

Senghor, L. S., *Prose and Poetry by Senghor*, ed. and trans. J. Reed and C. Wake (Oxford: Oxford University Press, 1964).

Senghor, L. S., *Nocturnes*, trans. J. Reed and C. Wake (London: Heinemann Educational Books, 1972).

Shringarpure, B., *Cold War Assemblages: Decolonization to Digital* (New York: Routledge, 2019).

Skinner, K., 'Agency and Analogy in African History: The Contribution of Extra-Mural Studies in Ghana', *History in Africa*, 34:1 (2007), 273–96.

Simmons, R., 'La pertinence de la poésie de David Diop pour les jeunes noirs aux Etats-unis', *Présence Africaine*, 75 (1970), 89–96.

Smith, L. T., *Decolonizing Methodologies: Research and Indigenous Peoples* (London: Zed Books, 1999).

Sousa Santos, B., *Epistemologies of the South: Justice against Epistemicide* (New York: Routledge, 2016).

Steemers, V., *Francophone African Narratives and the Anglo-American Book Market: Ferment on the Fringes* (New York: Lexington Books, 2021).

Suh, J. C., 'Methodological Issues Relating to Drama Translation Research in Cameroon', in E. N. Chia, J. C. Suh, and A. N. Tene, eds., *Perspectives on Translation and Interpretation in Cameroon* (Mankon, Bamenda: Langaa Research & Publishing, 2009), pp. 147–69.

Suhr-Sytsma, N., 'Theories of African Poetry', *New Literary History*, 50:4 (2019), 581–607.

Talento, S., 'Consecration, Deconsecration, and Reconsecration: The Shifting Role of Literary Translation into Swahili', in A. W. Khalifa, ed., *Translators Have Their Say? Translation and the Power of Agency* (Zurich: CETRA and Lit-Verlag, 2014), pp. 42–64.

Tamele, S., 'Developing a Publishing Infrastructure in Mozambique', *Words Without Borders*, January 2021, www.wordswithoutborders.org/article/january-2021-international-black-voices-developing-a-publishing-infrastruct (accessed 14 March 2021).

Tansi, S. L., *L'anté-peuple* (Paris: Éditions du Seuil, 1983).

Thierry, R., *Le marché du livre africain et ses dynamiques littéraires: Le cas du Cameroun* (Bordeaux: Presses universitaires de Bordeaux, 2015).

Tompkins, K. and Kinsella, T., 'Simon Mpondo', Stockton University website (n.d.), www.stockton.edu/stories/simon-mpondo.html (accessed 5 March 2021).

Toral, A., Wieling, M., and Way, A., 'Post-editing Effort of a Novel with Statistical and Neural Machine Translation', *Frontiers in Digital Humanities*, 5:9 (2018), 1–11.

Tuck, E. and Yang, K. W., 'Decolonization Is Not a Metaphor', *Decolonization: Indigeneity, Education & Society*, 1:1 (2012), 1–40.

Tymoczko, M. *Enlarging Translation, Empowering Translators* (Abingdon, UK: Routledge, 2007).

Ubanako, V. and Anderson, J., eds., *Crossing Linguistic Borders in Postcolonial Anglophone Africa* (Newcastle upon Type: Cambridge Scholars Publishing, 2014).

Vakunta, P., 'On Teaching the Translation of Hybrid African Literatures', *ASA Annual Meeting Paper* (2013), www.ssrn.com/abstract=2237241 (accessed 9 January 2021).

Venuti, L., *Contra Instrumentalism: A Translation Polemic* (Lincoln: University of Nebraska Press, 2019).

Venuti, L., *Translation Changes Everything: Theory and Practice* (Abingdon, UK: Routledge, 2013).

Vieira, E. R. P., 'Liberating Calibans: Readings of *Antropofagia* and Haroldo de Campos' Poetics of Transcreation', in S. Bassnett and H. Trivedi, eds., *Post-colonial Translation: Theory and Practice* (Abingdon, UK: Routledge, 1999), pp. 95–113.

Warner, T., *The Tongue-Tied Imagination: Decolonizing Literary Modernity in Senegal* (New York: Fordham University Press, 2020).

Washbourne, R. K., 'Teaching Literary Translation: Objectives, Epistemologies, and Methods for the Workshop', *Translation Review*, 86 (2013), 49–66.

Wells, N., Forsdick, C., Bradley, J. et al. 'Ethnography and Modern Languages', *Modern Languages Open*, 1:1 (2019), 1–16.

Wilder, G., *Freedom Time: Negritude, Decolonization, and the Future of the World* (Durham, NC: Duke University Press, 2015).

Wozny, D. and Cassin, B., eds., *Les intraduisibles du patrimoine en Afrique subsaharienne* (Paris: Demopolis, 2014).

Yesufu, A. R., 'A Note on David Diop's "Un berger" in *Le Temps du martyre*', *Meta: Journal des traducteurs*, 28:3 (1983), 308–10.

Zimudzi, T. B., 'Spies and Informers on Campus: Vetting, Surveillance and Deportation of Expatriate University Lecturers in Colonial Zimbabwe, 1954–1963', *Journal of Southern African Studies*, 33:1 (2007), 193–208.

Acknowledgements

David Diop's poem 'Défi à la force' is reproduced with permission of Présence Africaine. The English translations of the poem are reproduced with permission of Clive Wake and Indiana University Press. My thanks to Ray Ndébi for permission to reproduce an extract from his unpublished Camfranglais translation of Jane Austen's *Emma*.

This Element came together during the Covid pandemic and as I welcomed three children into the world. My warmest thanks go to collaborators, colleagues, friends, and family who have engaged generously with the ideas at various points and offered practical support and moments of joy throughout this period.

Cambridge Elements ☰

Publishing and Book Culture

SERIES EDITOR
Samantha Rayner
University College London

Samantha Rayner is Professor of Publishing and Book Cultures at UCL. She is also Director of UCL's Centre for Publishing, co-Director of the Bloomsbury CHAPTER (Communication History, Authorship, Publishing, Textual Editing and Reading) and co-Chair of the Bookselling Research Network.

ASSOCIATE EDITOR
Leah Tether
University of Bristol

Leah Tether is Professor of Medieval Literature and Publishing at the University of Bristol. With an academic background in medieval French and English literature and a professional background in trade publishing, Leah has combined her expertise and developed an international research profile in book and publishing history from manuscript to digital.

ADVISORY BOARD

Simone Murray, Monash University

Claire Squires, University of Stirling

Andrew Nash, University of London

Leslie Howsam, Ryerson University

David Finkelstein, University of Edinburgh

Alexis Weedon, University of Bedfordshire

Alan Staton, Booksellers Association

Angus Phillips, Oxford International Centre for Publishing

Richard Fisher, Yale University Press

John Maxwell, Simon Fraser University

Shafquat Towheed, The Open University

Jen McCall, Emerald Publishing

ABOUT THE SERIES

This series aims to fill the demand for easily accessible, quality texts available for teaching and research in the diverse and dynamic fields of Publishing and Book Culture. Rigorously researched and peer-reviewed Elements will be published under themes, or 'Gatherings'. These Elements should be the first check point for researchers or students working on that area of publishing and book trade history and practice: we hope that, situated so logically at Cambridge University Press, where academic publishing in the UK began, it will develop to create an unrivalled space where these histories and practices can be investigated and preserved.

Cambridge Elements ☰

Publishing and Book Culture
Colonial and Post-Colonial Publishing

Gathering Editor: Caroline Davis

Caroline Davis is Associate Professor in Publishing in the
Department of Information Studies at University College
London. She is the author of *Creating Postcolonial Literature:
African Writers and British Publishers* (Palgrave, 2013), the editor
of *Print Cultures: A Reader in Theory and Practice* (Macmillan,
2019) and co-editor of *The Book in Africa: Critical
Debates* (Palgrave, 2015).

A full series listing is available at: www.cambridge.org/EPBC

Printed in the United States
by Baker & Taylor Publisher Services